Not My Circus

Wisdom from an Old Ringmaster

CJ Corki

CJ Corki Publishing LLC
Lakewood, OH

CJ Corki/CJ Corki Publishing
132a Veterans Lane Suite #342
Doylestown, PA/18901
author@cjcorki.com

Publisher's Note: This is a work of fiction. Names, characters, places, and incidents are a product of the author's imagination or personal experiences. Locales and public names are sometimes used for atmospheric purposes. Any resemblance to actual people, living or dead, or to businesses, companies, events, institutions, or locales is completely coincidental.

Neither the author nor the publisher assumes any responsibility or liability on behalf of the consumer or reader of this material. Any perceived slight of any individual or organization is purely unintentional.

Book Cover Design 2023 - 100 Covers
Font: Open Dyslexic
Not My Circus/ CJ Corki-- 1st ed.

ISBN Hardcover: 979-8-9885588-0-4
ISBN Paperback: 979-8-9861397-9-1

Dedication

Cheers to our parents, Carl and Generose Szostak, the original ringmasters, who knew when to step down yet still passed on their invaluable wisdom and guidance through patience and understanding. Let's applaud them for their hard work and dedication.

TABLE OF CONTENTS

—————————————————————————————— Not My Circus

Opening

It's a different time, a different era for raising kids. As a grandparent, you have much to learn about this new-age circus. Even though you aren't the current ringmaster, your wisdom from yesteryear can benefit the rising generation. It is up to you to get out from behind the curtain and create your second act to make a difference in your grandkid's life.

> "This is brave; this is bruised
> This is who I'm meant to be, this is me"
> – The Greatest Showman

Your successes, as well as your failures, need to be shared. Everyone has a story. Take the journey with your grandkids to let them know your struggles growing up, difficulty with school, and life lessons you learned the hard way.

We shared our stories to get you started on the journey. It is a window into a simpler time before technology influenced our lives. As you begin to share those tales with your grandchildren, we've prompted you with talking points, books to share, and questions to ask. A page at the end of each chapter also includes a place to journal the experience.

We also compare the differences between eras as we struggle to keep up with the latest and greatest devices and trends. We dive into how generation gaps can impact relationships and show you practical strategies that will help strengthen bonds.

Using the foundation of the Polish Proverb: Not My Circus, Not My Monkeys, the Series is designed to share how we can raise our ability to shape and strengthen our grandchildren's lives through our values and guidance without the usual power that comes with the parent role. This role should always be considered.

You were raised under a different circus tent but learn how you can share your wisdom. Since this isn't your first circus, you have experience as an old ringmaster.

This book utilized a unique font, OpenDyslexic3. It makes it easier for both dyslexic and non-dyslexic readers to process. Dyslexia is a language-based learning difference that affects a person's ability to connect letters to sounds, making it difficult to read and spell. OpenDyslexic uses "heaviness," a typography technique that increases the visual weight of a typeface which helps prevent letters from turning upside down and therefore increases one's ability to distinguish individual letters while reducing reading errors and the overall effort it takes to read text.

So, step right up and embark on a thrilling journey through the enchanting world of grandparenting, where love, laughter, and magical moments steal the show under the big top of cherished memories.

1

A Different Circus

The time for action is now, it's never too late to do something. -Antoine de Saint-Exupery

Introduction

In today's rapidly changing world, the generational gap between us, as grandparents, and our grandkids can seem wider than ever before. However, this divide can also present a unique opportunity for us to play an indispensable role in our grandkids' growth. We grew up in a different era, shaped by diverse experiences yet armed with a wealth of wisdom. We possess insights that can enrich their lives. Like circus performers with various talents, we bring our unique skills, perspectives, and stories to the main tent of their grandkids' lives, creating a dynamic interplay of lessons, memories, and growth. Through our distinctive lens, we can nurture and guide our grandkids, offering invaluable support and sharing the remarkable gifts of our own circus with the next generation.

Not My Circus, Not My Monkeys Could Be a Fun Problem to Have

Did you know that circus monkeys are capuchin monkeys?

Capu....what? My memories of the circus were nothing so specific. To me, a monkey was a monkey but something unique, as if it was a creature from another planet. In addition, clowns, acrobats, and daredevils took my imagination to an exotic life of adventure and travel.

You may remember the movie, The Greatest Show on Earth, with Jimmy Stewart. It showed the dazzling spectacle of life behind the scenes with Ringling Bros.-Barnum and Bailey Circus.

After watching that movie numerous times and dreaming of a circus adventure, I finally had the opportunity to attend an extravagant three-ring circus.

You may not be aware of a Polish proverb, "Not my circus, not my monkeys," which translates to something we have no control over and do not want to be bothered with. Since it's rude and inconsiderate to say, "Not my problem," especially if someone is making an unreasonable request for your help, "it's funnier to say not my circus, not my monkeys." In Polish it is Nie mój cyrk, nie moje małpy. Humor-filled, yes. But still a great truth. Stay focused on what your concern is and stay focused on who your concern is. Don't get pulled into other people's stuff because sometimes, it's none of our business.

In the past, when I heard "not my circus," I saw a ringmaster and showman directing parts of a three-ring circus: performers, animals, workers, and equipment. The ringmaster had the whip and the authority to use it; with practiced ease, he signaled where everyone should be and where they should be performing. And those performers and animals all have agreed that they will pay attention to these messages from the ringmaster. They willingly participate in the circus, accepting directions to make the show work. But what if a stranger walked into that circus and tried to take over?

The protective gene naturally takes over and ensures that no disaster will follow. Confusion cannot reign, and the animals and performers go as planned. Even the clowns know their role.

So, why the analogy to a circus in this first chapter?

We all were once ringmasters of our own circus. This was ours when we were the parents. The responsibility to protect, develop, set rules, and discipline, when necessary, was ours and ours alone as the ringmaster.

Just like the circus that has evolved over the years into a more sophisticated entertainment experience, our circus has changed too. The new circus has too. This circus' ringmaster is new, young, and may have been influenced by your three-ring circus but is no longer ours.

Are you ready to be a part of another circus? You'll need to decide a few things, like what acts you want to include in your circus performance.

Even though we are now "an act," there is an opportunity to influence and entertain. We must define our roles and, of course, share them with the ringmaster.

Here are a few ideas of "acts" that can be memorable. With the younger ones, tents made from blankets and sheets could get their creative juices flowing. Popcorn and peanuts as snacks could be a yummy treat. Or if the weather is cooperating, and you have a play set in the backyard, you can amaze the audience with daring tricks with the monkey bars or swings. Do you know some card tricks, or can you juggle them? You want to include a fantastic animal act if you have a family pet. Perform for family members and all your neighbors. Sell popcorn and lemonade if you're ambitious and make it an event to remember. Collect the earned dollars and cents and put them into a piggy bank with plans to donate them to a local charity you all agree to help. Why a piggy bank? It's convenient, it's easy, and it can be educational. Use this opportunity as a teaching moment in math as you count the pennies, nickels, dimes, and quarters.

Remember, this is your "act," and the grandkids are your guest monkeys. You can be elevated to the main ring if you choose. It can be a fun problem to have.

Finally, going to the circus is still a source of inspiration and imagination for young and elder alike. If you dream of exotic places, thrilling adventures, and shared memories, grab a ticket, some cotton candy, and pass on this experience for future generations.

Just in case you were curious: Capuchin monkeys name comes from their coloration, which resembles the cowls worn by the Capuchin order of Roman Catholic friars.

Grandmother's Attic: Where memories and treasures of the past come alive

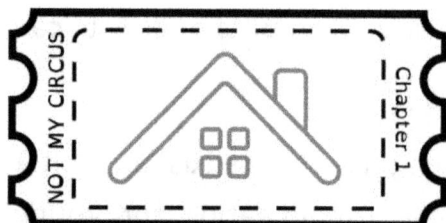

Have you ever wondered what your grandma's attic looks like and what secrets it holds? Well, this is your chance to find out! My mom's attic was a virtual space where we explored the hidden gems of a bygone era. From vintage clothing to antique furniture, there is something for everyone to discover in this nostalgic wonderland.

As my mind allows me to travel back in time, I remember trips with my daughters to my mom and dad's lake house in Illinois. When they were four and five, my mom, their grandmother, would entertain them by climbing up into the attic to retrieve and share the toys I grew up with as a child. As Grandfather creaked down the attic steps, he carefully brought down the toys, spread them out on the living room floor, and watched with amazement. All three sat on the floor for hours playing with Tinker toys, Lincoln Logs, and Legos. These building sets were a fun way for them to exercise their creativity and use their imagination. Connect 4 was a fan favorite and an exciting strategy game. Up off the floor and onto the kitchen table, they would continue their journey as they pull out a deck of cards and play Crazy Eights, a game that requires focus and patience; as you may know, in Crazy Eights, concentration is critical.

My dad, Grandfather, loved to tell stories and read my daughter's books. Books that were stored in the attic until the magical time when we came to visit. Hours were spent together reading as they teetered on Grandfather's rocking chair, listening intently to the beautiful stories.

Years later, when they were older, Grandmother taught the girls the game of Rummikub. A game that reinforced skills of sequencing, pattern recognition, and planning. I still enjoy playing this game with my daughters today.

In Grandmother's Attic, you can explore the past and gain a new appreciation for the things once cherished by those who came before us.

As my thoughts travel into the future, I envision my daughters visiting me with their boys and girls in tow. When that joyous day comes, I will entertain and play with the grandkids I dream about now. At this point, I don't know what they will be calling me. However, like their grandmother, I will retrieve the games and stuffed animals from their past stored in my attic.

So, take a step back in time and visit Grandmother's Attic. Whether you're a history buff, an antique lover, or simply looking for inspiration, this hidden gem has something for everyone. Take your chance to uncover past mysteries with your grandkids and make memories that will last a lifetime!
What toys are in your "Attic"?

Lessons From a Prior Generation: How to Be Great by Being a Great Aunt

NOT MY CIRCUS

Chapter 1

Maybe it isn't the status of being a grandparent, but being a Great Aunt plays a vital role in the life of a Great Niece or a Great Nephew. This responsibility should not be taken lightly. A great aunt can provide guidance, support, and love to their niece or nephew. They can also serve as a source of wisdom to demonstrate and teach the family's values.

Take, for instance, my Great Aunt, Aunt Kathryn. She was a formidable example of a caring but strong-willed and disciplined woman. She lost her husband only a year after she married in the 1920s. With no kids of her own, she dedicated her life to the family business. However, she was surrounded by her nieces and nephews, with whom she provided an example of good business practices and values.

We were in a retail business where lots of cash went in and out the door, from people buying the morning newspapers to cashing their weekly checks. Cash was abundant. I vividly remember stacks of money, from one-dollar bills to fifty, neatly stacked, all facing the same way. Some bills were even ironed to create a smooth stack to be counted meticulously.

Being surrounded by all that cash instilled a lesson in honesty. Although the money was precisely counted, what harm would it be to "borrow" a dollar or two? That was unanimously deemed unacceptable by my aunt, grandparents, and mom, who also worked there. Never would we even think about taking a dime, much less a dollar. She accurately accounted for each cent by counting it over and over and over. So precisely did she know the amount, even the bank couldn't match her preciseness when she caught many mistakes by the local branch down the street.

The lesson of responsibility started young. My aunt entrusted us to take thousands of dollars of cash to the bank down the street. As young as first grade, I carried a cloth bank sack filled with cash, coins, and checks to be deposited with our local savings and loan. The walk wasn't far, but we carried the bag discreetly to avoid potential theft. Another skill learned is awareness of surroundings for safety reasons.

She instilled the lesson of generosity. Since our parochial school was just across the street from the family store, we visited every day before and after school and often during lunch. Immediately after entering the store, she was there to greet us. She welcomed us with various available treats, from ice cream to candy. She gave with her heart and loved seeing our smiling faces as we sincerely thanked her for the tasty treats. This gesture also prompted our good manners to come through.

She ingrained my aunt's keen skill in organizing. When we could walk, we helped stock the shelves with goods. It started with candy, something that would interest a child, but moved into the entire store's inventory. Everything was to be neatly arranged and fully supplied. When items were low or out of stock, we knew how to reorder and were encouraged to do so. The concept of FIFO (First In, First Out) was introduced long before any business class.

I learned valuable lessons from my Great Aunt Kathryn that I hope to pass along to future generations: Honesty, Responsibility, Generosity, and Organization. A great aunt can play an essential role in a niece's or nephew's life by providing a loving and supportive presence, sharing family values, and offering guidance and advice when needed.

What would you like to pass along to the rising generation as a great Great Aunt?

Why Boredom is Key to Developing Creativity and Imagination in Children

Have you ever heard the dreaded, "I'm B-O-R-E-D!"

I have. To be transparent, I also said, "I'm B-O-R-E-D," a time or two in my childhood.

As adults, we often crave moments of stillness and quiet to escape from the hustle and bustle of our busy lives. However, when it comes to our children, we tend to fill their every waking moment with activities, playdates, and electronic devices to keep them occupied. While this may provide temporary relief for us grandparents and parents, studies suggest that kids need moments of boredom to foster creativity, imagination, and problem-solving skills.

So, how did my boredom problem get solved? Let me tell you a story. Growing up, we loved playing outside after school and before supper. Yep, supper, that's what someone from the mid-west called dinner...just in case you were curious. Anyway, I digress.

Our mother had a school bell she would ring that pierced the air and covered the entire neighborhood. When we heard it, we would drop whatever we were doing and go home. After supper, it was time to do homework, do evening chores (dishes), and, depending on the night, watch a favorite TV program before we went to bed.

But it was Sunday that I dreaded most. Why? We went to church in the morning, and Mom made a stomach-busting dinner for us afterward. We would then do the dishes, and our parents would put their feet up, dad in his rocking chair and mom on the couch, and they would take a much-deserved nap. We were left to our own devices.

We went outside and played with each other. Some of our friends and cousins in the neighborhood whose parents also were taking Sunday afternoon naps, but after a few hours, we were bored and returned home.

Once home, we had to be quiet since our parents were sleeping in the family room. So, what do we do? We put our heads together and often went to the hall, dragged out our Barbie dolls, and played with them. That quickly got boring...what next?

Our parents had no structured activities for us. They were asleep, and it was Sunday, and very little on TV was of interest to the children. When my dad woke from his nap, he would watch the TV program about WWII. He was fascinated with the historical footage since he was a WWII veteran, but we were not.

Being bored is very frustrating for a child since they don't know how to become un-bored.

Given the freedom to "figure it out." I solved my Sunday boredom by reading books. That was a quiet activity that didn't bother my napping parents. I discovered new worlds and new ideas. I enjoyed reading about the adventures of the Bobbsey Twins. I graduated to Nancy Drew mysteries, and there was probably a Hardy Boys book or two in the mix. I particularly liked Nancy Drew because she was a strong girl that bucked the day's morays about the role of a girl in using her head to solve mysteries. These books helped me to realize that a girl can be strong. I solved my own boredom.

But I digress. So, is it ok for the kids of today to be bored? I say emphatically, YES! We have grandkids in our lives with activities that take up every minute of their days. Gymnastics. Check. Team Sports. Check. Scouting. Check. I am not saying that activities aren't development opportunities, but when is too far? We don't allow them to be bored. Boredom can be a good downtime for anyone, child, and adult. TV off, social media off. No digital distractions.

As grandparents who have grown up with boring times, can you let your grandkids be bored when they visit you? Are you willing to take away their electronics? Unplug the TV? Let them have time at your house, left to their own devices, and see how they entertain themselves. Send them outside.

Do they know how to entertain themselves? Sure, there may be a grumble, but this may be the first time they have ever been bored and have had to think about what to do for themselves. Some may rebel or pout. Be strong. Kids are resourceful, and some may discover that downtime rejuvenates them. After an hour or two of boredom, you can lead them into your front room and introduce them to the 1000-piece puzzle you started...by design. This is something fun to finish. No electronics, only their own thinking.

A bored child is not bad; a bored child can open their mind to encourage their creative side. So, let's take our over-scheduled and over-stimulated kids and give them the gift of boredom. This gift is an opportunity rather than a burden.

Let us know how it goes!

A Worm-Hole

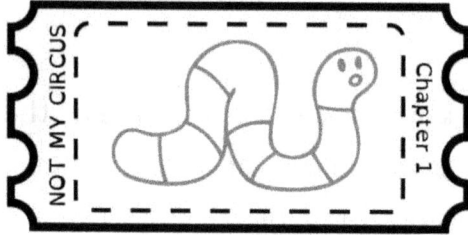

How about encouraging a budding entomologist? When I was a little girl, my dad and I would take walks around the block. After a rain one day, I saw some worms on the sidewalk and screamed. I feared these squirmy things keeping me from walking on the sidewalk. My father looked at me, took my hand, and ushered me to the grass beside the sidewalk. He said, "Wait here." He walked over, and to my horror, he picked up one of these squirmy vermin. The worm wrapped itself around dads' finger as he showed it to me. "Princess, this is a worm. They won't hurt you. I recoiled from his hand. Then Dad petted the worm. "Touch it," he said. "It won't hurt you. He transferred the worm to his hand and held it out to me. I shook my head. No way I was going to touch this thing.

Dad didn't force me to touch it. Instead, he stroked it and told me, "Worms are essential, and they take care of our garden.

I looked at him with wide eyes. "They take care of our garden. How?"

He chuckled and said, "They burrow in the soil and make it easier for the plants to grow because the soil is loose. Let's go home and check out our tomato plants."

We walked back to the house. My father and I ensured we did not step on any worms on the sidewalk. He took his trowel to the soil around our tomato plants. "See how many worms are here?" I tried to count them, but Dad said, "They are important for our garden. Don't be afraid of them. They won't hurt you. They will make sure we have big red tomatoes to eat."

I learned my lesson. The next day, after it rained, I went out and picked up all the worms from the sidewalk, put them in my pocket, and brought them back to my dad.

"I saved them," I said, stuck my hand in my pocket, and pulled out a handful of worms. My father couldn't stop laughing. "So what do you want to do with them?" he asked. "Let's put them in the garden, so our tomatoes grow well."
We did that.

As grandparents, we can introduce nature to our grandchildren even if everyone lives in the city or suburbs. It is as simple as introducing them to worms. You can teach your grandchildren not to fear or hurt them and explain why they are essential to the environment. Unlike when I was a child, as a grandparent, you can join your grandchild to search online about worms and their value and explore what worms add to the environment.

What was the first bug you were introduced to when you were little? Were you taught not to fear it? A fascination for bugs and worms introduces your grandchildren to entomology, studying bugs. Who knows, they may want to learn more. You, as grandparents, can be the catalyst for your grandchildren's future.

If I Could Save Time in a Bottle

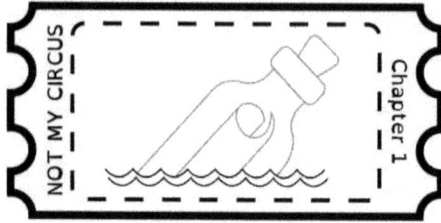

If you opened a time capsule from 1971, what would you find?

One of the many things I hope to find is an old vinyl record by Jim Croce, who wrote the soulful song, *Time in a Bottle*. How many remember it? Here is a teaser of how it began as I take you down memory lane...

If I could save time in a bottle
The first thing that I'd like to do
Is to save every day 'til eternity passes away
To spend them with you

These few lines of the song can awaken many different memories depending on where we are.

Some might see it as an old geezer song from the past, others a memory from a college night contemplating a hopeful future. Still others, like Jim Croce, wrote this reflective song the night he found out his wife was pregnant. The couple had been married for five years, and after meeting with a fertility specialist, the outcome was a baby. The joy was palpable. The new addition, the promises of a bright future, the exciting venture into a world of possibilities, and then less than two years later, Jim Croce's life was tragically cut short by a plane crash.

We all know that no one has a crystal ball for the future. As the song so aptly continues:
But there never seems to be enough time
To do the things you want to do once, you find them

Our family's experiences and achievements serve as a source of inspiration and guidance for future generations. It holds immense importance in the lives of families. It also plays a vital role in shaping one's identity, values, and sense of belonging.

Ahhh, memory lane. We all have them. It may be 1989, 2000, 2010, or anything in-between.

This trip down memory lane is because we have earned the historian's level. As elders, grandparents hold the key to the family's history and can offer grandchildren insight into their heritage, providing a sense of belonging. The role of a historian is ours, and the holiday season is a great time to dust off those history books. The low-hanging fruit is telling stories at Christmas Eve dinner, making cookies, caroling, and visiting neighbors on Christmas Day. Tell stories about yourself, relatives, events, and family traditions.

My most memorable Christmas tradition was spending Christmas Eve in the basement of Auntie Jean's house. We all knew the holiday spirit and music could be heard as we entered the house. Down the dark stairs, we were greeted with hugs, hi's, and lots of love. A minimum of 50 people constantly came and went with cousins, aunts, uncles, and of course, the visiting Santa Claus, all celebrating the joyous night. Before midnight mass, there was enough food for every taste bud. Roast Beef. Check. Pierogi. Check. Dill

Pickles. Check. Ham. Check—casseroles of every type and size. Check. The food was endless, with a focus on our traditional Polish fare.

The family was extensive, so as we aged out of the "kid's table," we moved to sit at the bar talking about college, life, and future dreams, and every one of us never thought this would ever end. Ask any of them, and their memory of Christmas Eve is still as vivid and memorable.

What is your favorite memory from your childhood? Have you shared it with the grandkids? In addition to sharing history, make some history together too. Create memories of your own.
My family has stepped it up and added a family time capsule into our tradition.

A family time capsule allows you to preserve the time that is so quickly slipping through your fingers. Even if you don't think so now, you will miss the days your grandkids tracked snow through the house. A time capsule can offer a fond memory of those sweet days. Please share it and have them open it in 10 years. Some ideas include:

- Share pictures, old family recipes, and newspaper clips
- Stories from a family trip or activity
- Create a family tree with pictures

As Jim Croce said:
If I had a box, just for wishes
And dreams that had never come true
The box would be empty
Except for the memory of how you answered
them

Let's change that paradigm and fill that box with stories so they won't be empty.

I hope that when my grandkids think of me, the final line from the song will help them remember me.

I've looked around enough to know.
That you're the one I want to go through time
with.

Wishing you and your family years of memories splashed with some history that will go through time with the next generation.

FUN THINGS TO DO

Talk:

TALK about how the past is like a puzzle. It shows us where we've been and as they collect those puzzle pieces from you it will make them wiser and it will help them grow and become even more amazing!
Every family has stories, and those stories you are sharing are a chests of wisdom about how life was before and how it is always changing.

Recommend to Read:

- Patrick Picklebottom and the Longest Wait - Mr Jay & Gary Wilkinson

- Imagine a World: Filled with Wonder - Heather Lean

- Dear Girl You are Amazing - Emily Green

Questions to Ask:

What is something new you would like to try? Why does it interest you?

How do you think you can prepare yourself to try this new thing?

Tell me of a time when you tried something new and it was a little difficult at first, but then you got better at it?

CORE VALUE: GROWTH

The world needs more dreamers, innovators, and rebels who dare to challenge the status quo and make a difference.

Stories:

Books:

Questions Asked:

2

Boomers Failures, Lessons Learned

We had 'social networking' back in the day, it was called 'go out and play.' - Auntie Acid

Introduction

In a world that's quick to celebrate successes, we must recognize the valuable role that failure plays in shaping our lives. We, as Boomers, have experienced both the soaring highs of success and the crushing lows of setbacks. But it's from these moments of failure that we've gained the most wisdom – lessons that we're eager to pass on to our cherished grandkids.

Our extensive life experience has given us many insights into what it takes to triumph over adversity. We want nothing more than to share these hard-earned pearls of wisdom with the next generation, arming them with the tools they need to navigate the challenges that lie ahead. By recounting our own stories of resilience, determination, and growth, we can equip them with a profound understanding that, even in the face of failure, there's always something valuable to be learned – and that anything is achievable with the right mindset.

Let's Make This a Year of Failure

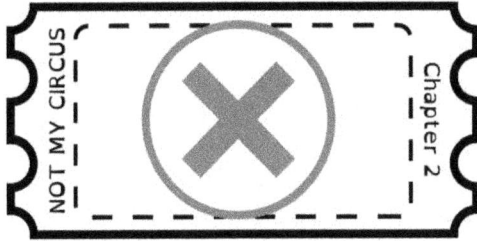

Are you looking for success for your grandkids? If so, stop reading now.

As we begin a new year, we typically contemplate the changes or enhancements we want to focus on in our upcoming year. You and I probably already have our "to do's or "to change" list ready. The typical list begins with losing weight, exercising, saving money, spending more time with family and friends...

I am not saying that these aspirations shouldn't be thought about...for you and me. However, I believe the resolution that should support your grandkids is a failure. Yes, failure. Most kids are afraid to fail, and we want them to succeed. What if we recognized that failure is good and an essential step in their development? When kids fail, amazing things can happen for them (and us).

You might be asking...why?

Why? Because it appears that our grandkids are growing up with fewer challenges, obstacles, and worries. They are in a safer setting than ever before. Now you may be thinking about the horrific drive-by shootings, the dangers of the streets, the human trafficking, and all the other safety issues that keep adults up at night. Yes, they are very real and should be addressed. Instead, what I am referring to is the fundamentals. You know, Maslow's Hierarchy of needs theory. No, this isn't an academic discussion, but instead wanted to say that most of our grandkids do not hunger for food...ever, have a roof over their heads, more clothes than most 3rd world countries, and probably have the internet at their fingertips.

Surrounded by this safety net allows them, more than any other generation, a chance to try new things, early and often...and to fail. Let's help them on this journey.

So, how do they fail? It starts with thinking about what they want to do or try that they have never done before. Love sports? Try a sport that is not a mainstream activity...how about dressage?

I love to read. Write a book.

Not all the challenges have to be a big "C"; a little "c" challenge can start the thought process. How about a blindfold challenge? Trying an activity without the use of your eyes. Have your little ones try to draw a picture without seeing the paper or accomplish something new in seven seconds. The seven-second challenge can include the following:

- Sing the letters of the alphabet backward
- What is the number before 1 trillion?
- Name five foods that end with the letter 'y'

How can we support them in this endeavor? Celebrate failure! Yep, here are a few ideas on how to support them:

- Allow them to brag about their failure.
- Maybe have a "Failure Friday" where all failures are heard.
- Failing forward is a business concept that fits here perfectly. What this means is learning from your errors. Ask questions like, "What did you learn from this? or "What would you do differently next time?" Shift focus on the positive aspects of failure.

Anything worth doing is difficult, and failure is part of the process. Think about your biggest mistakes. They taught you more courage, strength, and wisdom than any success could have. Instead of letting kids fear failure, we can help them see it as a learning opportunity.

So, join me on this journey of failure. Let us know what you decide to do. We would love to hear your failure stories.

How I Survived My Childhood

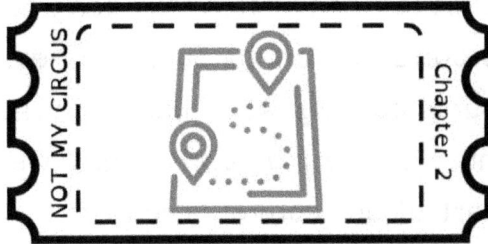

NOT MY CIRCUS

Chapter 2

As a kid, I was always excited to learn new words. We were fortunate that, with a mere 18 payments, our family would be a proud owner of the World book encyclopedia set. The door-to-door salesman said that it was written in layman's English and designed to cover significant areas of knowledge with a particular focus on science, technology, and medicine. We had the world at our fingertips.

Once a year, around six months in, a package wrapped in brown paper arrived. The coveted new "book of the year" was here. Of course, the information provided was about what occurred over the last year, but it was jam-packed with facts, pictures, history, and global news. We hungrily unwrapped our prize possession, and the three eldest lay on the floor, gingerly turning the pages as ooh's and ahhhs could be heard, as we spent hours learning what had happened in our world and discovering words that were not a normal part of our conversations.

Between the arrival of our yearly book, we still wanted to continue learning. So, the dictionary was a well-worn friend. One day we heard a word at school that intrigued us and was never said in our household. So, to the dictionary we went. Wanting to sound continental and be "with it," we figured we should incorporate the word into our vocabulary. This single word would be a word that would show our maturity. Turning the pages to "b," we were perplexed. Hmmm, it sure didn't make any sense. Webster's definition was (noun) the female of the dog.... Why would someone say that to a friend?

Critical thinking may not have been our strong suit during our early years. Later that day, we were in the living room, and my sister said something that irked me, and I called her THAT word. She was shocked and provoked and yelled back to me, "You B-I-T-*-H," although our dad heard it this time. I never saw him move so fast. A man who never raised his voice started yelling about how that was a bad word; she should never say it to anyone; he asked who taught her that word and that he would wash her mouth out with soap, all without taking a breath.

Through tears, of course, she said I said it first. The best defense is typically a good offense, but my dad would have none of it. Our quick lesson was that we should have looked past the first definition. If so, we would have found Webster to tell us: a malicious, spiteful, or overbearing woman, used as a generalized term of abuse and disparagement for a woman.

Kids' fascination with taboo words isn't new, of course. Around 5 or 6, most kids get a big thrill out of forbidden words. The definition of curse or "swear" words, based on dictionary.com, is "the expression that a wish of misfortune, evil, or doom befall a person..." Instead of the use of soap to help your grandkids understand that there are better words they can use to substitute for a curse word, here are a few thoughts:

1. Check yourself...do swear words roll trippingly off your tongue? If so, now may be a great time to find alternative words; we are also "our message."

2. Purchase a thesaurus to help them find other words to convey their message better.

3. Ask them how they would feel if someone used that word on them. Sometimes just thinking about how being the recipient helps them understand the sting. Just like it's not OK to hit or bully someone, it's not OK to curse at someone to hurt them.

4. Language choices reflect on them. Remind them that "they" are the message. What they say and what they do can quickly become their brand. Someone who curses a lot tends to look immature and not at all classy.

So, help your grandkids understand that words are powerful and that certain words make a significant impact.

What was your first taboo word? What was your
punishment? CJ Corki would love to hear.

BTW- I did say it first...

Scrabble: TOAD vs. TODE: Imagination at its Finest

How do YOU spell T-O-A-D?

According to Wikipedia, "Scrabble is a word game in which two to four players score points by placing tiles, each bearing a single letter, onto a game board divided into a 15×15 grid of squares. The tiles must form words that, in crossword fashion, read left to right in rows or downward in columns and be included in a standard dictionary." Research shows that playing games can improve children's abilities to organize, plan and get along with others. In addition, play helps with language, math, and social skills and helps children cope with stress.

Well, not sure about the stress part...

So, why my question? Many years ago, my cousin and I were innocently playing Scrabble, and I came up with the word TODE with my letter tiles. I thought that was how you really did spell TOAD. An honest mistake. Kind of. Since that day, it has been a standing joke in my family. The good news is that my spelling skills have greatly improved, but that is one event I can never live down. My cousin has been sending me toad paraphernalia ever since; I have so many toad-like ornaments that I could decorate an entire Christmas tree. Thank you, Cousin Renee.

Einstein said, "Imagination is more important than knowledge." Imagination is the door to possibilities. Creativity, ingenuity, and thinking outside the box, or lines, begin for child development.

Imaginative and creative play is how children learn about the world. Children express themselves verbally and non-verbally during imaginative play, plan, interact, act, react, and try different roles.

So, how can we help? Great learning opportunities are possible when children participate in creative play with boxes, blocks, rocks, or dolls. I am sure you can get an Amazon box or two.

Also, creatively thinking while manipulating playdough, creating recipes by mixing dirt and water, splashing in puddles, working with art materials, or pretending to fly can further their development.

Imagination and creativity at a young age are just a steppingstone that our children will eventually need when they join the workforce.

One of my other favorite activities was playing house in our basement with my younger sister, with our father's handmade kitchen set bringing back fun memories. The funny thing is that neither of us cooks as adults; lucky for us, our husbands do a marvelous job putting food on our tables.

Children who witness adults being caring and nurturing will want to emulate that. Playing house can help foster a child's respect for the household chores they see their parents performing. It's okay not to have fancy equipment for playing house. Kids can imagine various household scenarios with just the blankets and chairs in the family room, make a tent, and even use everyday items they see you using. How about handing them some writing paper and a pen? They can take your lunch order pretending to serve you a meal. Likely they will end up making more of a mess in the process, but let it happen.

Another easy activity is opening your closet and letting them play "dress up." Dressing in costumes can spark a kid's imagination as well. Not your closet? A costume box or drawer at home allows your kids to experiment with different characters and act out plays. You can use old clothes, props, accessories, or lengths of fabric. Their old Halloween costumes and old, deflated soccer balls as head attire are handy for this favorite activity. The sky is the limit, and you can get creative with them.

Kids stretch their imaginations during play, and playing board games, like Scrabble, is one easy way. They create make-believe games or get lost in pretend worlds. A swing set can send them off to a fantasy land where Ishkabibble's roamed, and they can act out different solutions while boosting their confidence. They make their own rules and learn to follow or adapt them. These are valuable skills for navigating life and developing relationships with others or giving them special memories.

These skills bring back fond memories of playing with my sisters and cousin Renee.

Toad or Tode, how do you creatively spell it?

School Lunches: What it Says About You, Your Family, and Where You Live

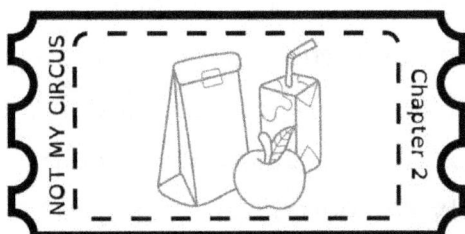

What assessments have you taken to determine your personality, communication style, or strengths? As a "boomer," we have taken most of them. What about you?

Was it Meyer Briggs, Gallup's Strength Finders, or DISC? Did you know what you had for lunch as a kid could also tell you lots about yourself? Peanut Butter and Jelly or Bologna with Mayonnaise were common options for a Baby Boomer. Take peanut butter, for example. Do you like crunchy or smooth? Did you know that people that prefer crunchy peanut butter consider themselves optimists?

Jelly could consist of a staple like grape, strawberry, or elaborate like raspberry preserves. Grape jelly, according to Google, says you're traditional and reliable. You prefer to stick with what you know works and don't like taking unnecessary risks. Strawberry jelly implies you are friendly and outgoing. You enjoy being around people and are often the life of the party. If you prefer raspberry, you are considered sophisticated and refined. You have a taste for the finer things in life and enjoy indulging in them.

What about the bread? Did you have white bread like Wonder bread or whole wheat? White represents comfort and familiarity. Wonder Bread is associated explicitly with cost-conscious families. However, whole wheat, which wasn't popular until the 1970s, represents health consciousness and a desire for a balanced diet. It's often preferred by families who prioritize eating natural ingredients.

But another option, Bologna, is an exciting lunch alternative. Bologna is considered the budget lunch. It is relatively inexpensive to purchase and highly convenient for busy parents. Those families choosing this option are not necessarily health conscious but rather convenience aware. If kids choose this lunch staple, it is more about comfort food than the preference for taste and texture. For many families, it symbolized assimilation or integration for those in the Italian American community. And as I can confirm, it was also integration for the Polish-American community.

Let's talk condiments. What condiment to choose for the bologna sandwich? Mayonnaise, yes, but which brand? The big-name rivals are Hellmann's vs. Miracle Whip. I grew up with Miracle Whip. Preferences seem to be regional, but those more health-conscious prefer Hellmann's. But if you choose bologna, I suspect most sandwiches have Miracle Whip for these cost-sensitive families.

Although nostalgia reflects these two staple choices for lunch in the 1960s and 1970s, fast forward to the 1990s, this period introduced

Lunchables. As a mother of three, this was a game changer. Who has time to get all the ingredients in a lunch bag: bread, peanut butter, jelly, chips, and juice? And then prepare lunch in the morning while getting the kids ready for school. A pre-prepared solution was the genius of Oscar Meyer. I joke that the boom of Charcuterie boards was due to this age group being exposed to Lunchables growing up. So, from the point of parental convenience to sophistication, it says you have developed a more adventurous palate.

In the 2020s, sandwiches are still the primary entrée, but wraps have become popular instead of sandwich bread. With more awareness of gluten, this alternative has skyrocketed as the center of lunch. Included are tomatoes, lettuce, cucumber, and hummus without the soggy mess of using white bread. Sides of fruit or vegetables and yogurt or cheese are common. And the drink? Water ranks the highest in preferences for parents to include. And if a parent included a special treat, it would be trail mix. Is this trend making the next generation more health-conscious or more cautious? The verdict is still out.

What you had for lunch is also a reflection of what state you live in. California, New York, Connecticut, and Minnesota are noted for the healthiest school lunches due to their policies on health and wellness. However, Mississippi, Alabama, and Louisiana due to the availability of unhealthy alternatives at the schools themselves. I understand parents' frustration with these competitive options since our school had sodas available for my kids as an alternative to the juice I provided. But is taking away this option taking away the freedom of choice?

Lunch selections can reflect taste preferences, cultural background, where you grew up, and when. What you bring to school reflects your family's health-consciousness awareness vs. price sensitivity. It can even reflect the parent's or child's willingness to try various foods. In my case, I loved SpaghettiOs growing up, for lunch and dinner. And reflecting on my assessment tests would also remember that I don't like change.

Think about what foods you had for lunch growing up. What does it say about you? What foods do you consider comfort foods today? Do they bring back memories from your youth? My comfort food is a gluten-free butter less grilled cheese sandwich with organic tomato soup. The details are different, but the memories are the same. One of my Strengthfinder strengths, Discipline. That matches my lunch choice. What about you? Do your childhood lunch choices mirror your assessments?

Mine...no MINE!

We haven't ever heard THAT said before, have we? Of course not! But if we are honest with ourselves, chances are that we can remember a time or two that we said it during our childhood. Be honest...I won't tell. After all, I, too, can vividly remember many times. I invited my teddy bears, bunnies, stuffed animals, and coveted doll to my tea party. My sister decided my doll didn't need to be part of my elaborate festivity and was whisked away for another adventure.

You may recall I grew up with four siblings, so yours, mine often became ours, but not without a few choice tantrums.

Learning how to play fair and being kind and respectful is a must at this stage of development and is an essential social skill that 1–4-year-olds are exposed to with others their age at school, during playdates, or with their siblings.

If toddlers are in the house, their cooperating and sharing skills may be challenged. You may have noticed that the test began during Halloween trick or treating. The popular candy in your siblings' bowl and not yours... Mine. Thanksgiving, who will get the window seat as we drive to Grandmother's house or sit on Mommy's lap...Mine. This challenge continues even to Christmas. That is another 30 days of Mine...Mine...Mine.

So, how can we help them stay on the development track? After all, at this point, they can walk, talk, and explore. They are somewhat independent throughout the day, so we know they can understand. We can help them settle down and help them retain what they started to learn by cooperating and sharing.

Here are a few ideas that might be fun for both of you:

- **Giving** – even with only a few short years under their belt, there are probably a few clothes they have outgrown and are sitting in the back of the closet. Maybe there are "baby" toys sitting in the toy box that are often overlooked. Work together and sort through what could be donated. As they are making decisions on what should stay and what should go, share with them why this is an essential and lifelong activity that should take place. If they struggle to understand the why, the book Socks for Christmas by Andy Andrews will give a touching, funny, and heartwarming explanation.

- **Follow the Leader** – A simple game packed with learning opportunities. The rules are simple: It starts with a child chosen to be the leader; the rest of the kids line up behind the leader. They must copy all the actions and movements of the leader (run, jumping jacks, clapping, whatever the leader does, they do. If someone doesn't successfully copy a move, they are out. The leader in the next round is the last child still following at the end.

- **Role-play** - Kids love to pretend. One easy, fun role-play is taking on a person or animal's role and acting out a scenario. Some ideas:

- Act out what the other person might feel when someone takes something away. Young kids are fascinated with superheroes. They could pretend to be a superhero and what they would do to make the sad child happy without getting the item back.

- Act like mommy and daddy and act out how they would handle the situation. These are just a few role-play topics you can try to introduce, but there are ideas everywhere around us. The only limit is your imagination. As they walk in someone else's shoes, they learn empathy and develop insight into how people act and feel.

Let's play some games that are easy to follow and have a lesson embedded in them, and are surrounded by lots of fun.

For the Love of a Tomato

Did you help your parents with a vegetable garden when you were young?

My dad loved to garden and would plant tomatoes every year. When I was little, he asked me if I would help him.

We started at the local hardware store and bought a packet of tomato seeds, which cost 15 cents. Dad showed me how to take some potting soil (he always kept some in his garden shed) and fill the egg holders of a used egg carton mother gave us instead of throwing it out. He showed me how to take a tiny individual seed and plant it. A challenge for a little child's hands. After washing out the residue ammonia, we then took a glass cleaner pump sprayer that Mother gave us. Did I mention that we reused things instead of buying new ones? We filled it with water and wet down the soil. "Spray gently, you need not disturb the seeds, but they need water to grow." We put the egg carton on the sunny windowsill over the kitchen sink.

"Now we wait." Of course, I was too excited to wait and would run to the kitchen every morning to check the egg carton and back again after I came home from school. I was getting impatient after nothing seemed to happen after three days. Daddy said, "Patience, it takes time." Then one morning, I saw little green shoots breaking through the soil.

We watched the little shoots grow into baby tomato plants. I started crying because only 9 of the 12 plants sprouted. "Sweetie, you will learn that not everything does what you want. You have nine beautiful plants. Be proud of your success."

One day Dad said, "Don't you think we need to give these seedlings more room to grow?" I nodded solemnly. We went to the garden shed and found some small clay pots he kept there. "We will move the seedlings to the shed, and Mother doesn't like to have all the dirt in her kitchen." He gave me a conspiratorial wink.

We transferred the seedlings to the pots and put them under a fluorescent light Daddy had set up in the shed. Every day I watched the seedlings grow.

"Now we plant," Dad said one day. And we did. And we watched the tomato plants grow. He taught me how to stake the plants so they didn't fall over and how to pinch off the suckers. "These suckers will make more leaves but not more tomatoes. It would be best if you had plants to reach the sun. That is why we stake them."

The lessons continued as he taught me to fertilize and watch the flowers turn into baby tomatoes and grow into big tomatoes. Daddy explained to me about the bees pollinating the flowers. I was amazed. It took time, and I was not used to waiting. Frustrating.

But then we picked the first tomato. Dad had me like it. I was so excited. It was a moment I would never forget. We brought it into the kitchen, and Mother cut it into slices and put it on two plates. Dad handed me the saltshaker, and he and I ate the tomato. The tomato that I grew.

Over the years, my patience improved under his guidance. I learned that good things take time and that nothing always goes perfectly. Thank you, Daddy.

How about teaching your grandchild to grow a tomato plant? You may "sprout" a memory or two.

No space? Planting can be done in a container as there are compact patio tomatoes. You can start them in a sunny window. It is good to start them with a seed so your grandchildren learn disappointment if their origin doesn't grow. Teach them how to nurture and feed their tomato plant and deal with forgetting to water their plant. A tomato plant is a responsibility. Teach them early.

Your grandchildren may never have to raise a tomato plant to keep from starving (an issue during MY grandparents' time because a garden kept food on their table during WWII. Their parents survived the Great Depression, relying on a garden.

Growing food will teach our grandkids patience and understanding that expectations don't always come through and that perseverance gets you, including failure if their plant dies. A packet of seeds now costs $2, but what an invaluable investment in your grandchild. And don't forget to teach them the value of using things on hand, like egg cartons, to start their seeds. Teach them some history, such as the role of Victory Gardens during WWII.

Do you live across the country from your grandchildren? Not a problem. Involve the parents and have them take pictures with their smartphones and text the photos to you every day while your grandchild is nurturing their tomato plant. You can face-time your grandchild to hear about their experiences as they grow their tomato plant. Revel in their success, and console them for setbacks. Encourage them to research if their tomato shows blossom-end rot and what to do about it. Parents can be busy with their jobs and getting the kids to and from school and afterschool activities and may not think about something as simple as growing a tomato plant, but you can become your grandchildren's influencer.

What is your tomato story? What did you learn as a child that you passed on to your grandkids?

There is Just Something About a Red Solo Cup

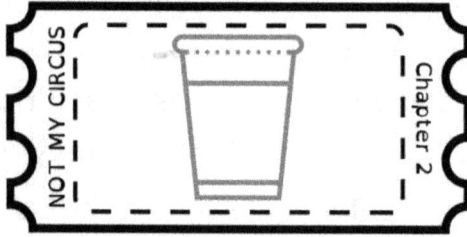

NOT MY CIRCUS

Chapter 2

Grandparents....OMG, they are sooooo old.

The word "grandparent" conjures up a picture in our mind's eye of a slightly bent-over, grey-haired person, moving as if every step is calculated and painful. We see a roadmap of lines that tell the story of their decades of living. Others might picture Jane Fonda (84) or Lily Tomlin (82) from Netflix's Grace, and Frankie, someone with vigor, cutting-edge wit, and great wisdom. They appear to have endless energy and lineless faces either by great family genes or a fantastic plastic surgeon looking half their age. Both types bring insight, observation skills, and the time to help their grandkids be all they can be.

So, what does this shoutout on grandparents have to do with red solo cups? These disposable cups came into popularity in the 1970s, during the time when the practice of sharing glasses and communal cups was normal behavior when the public realized that disposable cups weren't germ-ridden disease transmitters.

Any college student from the 70s till now knows and has used the red solo cup. Some of you may have too. Limited only by your imagination, a red solo cup became a popular beer pong game on college campuses and retirement communities. How about the perfect Jell-O mold or a stackable bowling game?

My favorite use for these red objects is for the popular shell game. Starting with three cups set down in line with one ball visible and then secretly placed beneath one cup, moving it around to "trick" the player. The game's object is to guess correctly which cup the ball is hidden under. Our mental and visual skills are challenged as it is maneuvered and quickly moved around. We must really pay attention.

To be a successful grandparent, I see our interaction with our grandkids as a real-life shell game. Our role is to closely watch those moving signs (the red solo cups) and decipher where our grandkids are (the ping pong ball) at that moment. The parents have a lot on their plate. During our interaction, if we observe, read the signs, and figure out where they are at that moment, we can help provide guidance and support. Are they anxious? Are they curious? Are they ready to learn about traditions? Are they looking to escape? Are they just having fun?

As with the shell game, we can sometimes miscalculate which cup the ball is under (where our grandkids are), so what do we do?

Shuffle the cups and look again for success. After all, with persistence, focus, and experience, we might get it right the next time or learn "tells," so we are ready to find where the ball (our grandkids) is.

So, raise your red solo cup to all grandparents out there who will continue to play the shell game as we make a subtle mark on creating the next generation.

If you are looking for red solo cup activities, you can always visit our website.

FUN THINGS TO DO

Talk:

Share examples of how errors and failing at something happens to everyone. Tell them about mistakes you have made and what you learned from them. Talk about how mistakes will make them better and that the mistakes teach them how to solve problems, how to bounce back when things go bad and learn that everything will still be ok.

Recommend to Read:

- Oh the Places You will Go - Dr. Seuss

- Ricky, the Rock that Couldn't Roll - Mr. Jay and Erin Wozniak

- Steve, the Dung Beetle: On a Roll - Susan Stoltz

Questions to Ask:

Can you think of a time when you tried something new and it didn't go as planned? How did you feel about it?

How can we learn from our mistakes? What can we do differently next time to get a different result?

What is something you are curious about and would like to learn more about?

CORE VALUE: KNOWLEDGE

Without the knowledge of our past history, origin and culture is like a tree without roots.

Stories:

Books:

Questions Asked:

3

Minding Our Ps and Qs: Nurturing Polite and Respectful Behavior

"Knowledge will give you power, but character respect."
Bruce Lee

Introduction

This chapter explores how influential YOU can be in shaping the behavior of young minds! This chapter explores how we can influence and teach manners, self-respect, and kindness – three powerful tools for a brighter future.

We can guide and demonstrate the importance of polite and empathetic behavior by just having them observe us. Let's show them how a simple "please" and "thank you" can brighten someone's day or how a heartfelt apology can mend misunderstandings.

So, join us as we continue this journey together. Our love, guidance, and lessons will contribute to sculpting grandkids and eventually, the world where unity and positivity rule. Here are a few stories that might spark some of your own ideas.

Redefining Manners

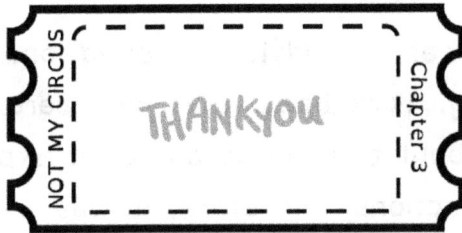

NOT MY CIRCUS | THANKYOU | Chapter 3

What are some of your etiquette lessons? We'd love to know.

Did you ever have a time when you weren't sure what was the "proper" way to act was? Do we shake hands now? Do we open the door for someone? What do you think is "right?"

For me, my dilemma's growing up were Which fork do I use? How do I address an adult? Do I have to say please? What about thank you? Writing thank you notes...why?

I will tell you that these are things that I didn't know I needed to know. As a kid, I was playing, climbing, roller skating, and mostly interacting with other kids. Which fork did I use? The one that was on the table...I wasn't a neanderthal!

However, as an adult, I looked back on my upbringing. I realized that my parents were serious about training us on social expectations and interactions; therefore, it was part of our daily life lessons.

I wish I could go back in time to ask why the etiquette choices they decided were non-negotiable, but my research shows that Miss Manners is not only a real thing but a real person. Yes, Judith Martin, in her 80's now, has been a syndicated "authority" on manners since 1978 and there was Emily Post before then. Did they read her column, or did they use their personal experiences to identify what was critical to our social success?

The fundamentals are that good manners show that you value the feelings of others. There is probably 50+ behaviors that we were expected to learn when I was growing up. There was probably 30+ that were identified and expected behavior from my kids. Now, as a grandparent, I must ask myself how many expected social behaviors are expected from the next generation.

One vivid memory I had growing up was from every Thanksgiving as far back as I can remember. We went to my mom's brother's house with grandparents, adults, and 13 kids, the chance of making it to the "adult table" was a slim possibility. Even though we were relegated to the "kids table," the use of multiple forks, spoons, and glasses took the celebration to a new level. Why the first fork? When not to use the first fork, and just when you think you survived the class, the following Thanksgiving, I found myself facing a quiz year after year. Of course, this holiday was the only time, as a kid, I had come across this utensil. To a kid, a 364-day break does not retention make. To this day, every time I see that first fork, I get a cold sweat and wonder if I will make it past that first test.

As for the topic of how to address an adult, as a kid, it was easy. An adult was either aunt or uncle X (first name), non-family were still aunt or uncles, and casual adult interaction was always

Mr. or Mrs. X (last name). Easy, until I became an adult myself, and I had to talk to slightly older adults, like my first boss. Do you want to know how hard it was to not call him Mr. Gully and call him Harold instead? Weird. The rules for my kids on the naming procedure were still aunt or uncle, for the real aunts or uncles, or Miss X (first name) for friends. There was one exception, and that was my brother-in-law, Tom. You can guess why he only wanted his first name used. Of course, you can always just call him "Tom my uncle," which his nephews do! Really...to this day! Creative etiquette...love it.

Research from the Emily Post Etiquette Institute has shown that the following generation's etiquette on calling a person a specific name is whatever the recipient wants to be called. Defaulting to the formal is always appropriate until told otherwise, so things here haven't appeared to change too much.

Let's spend a moment talking about please and thank you. These are probably the 3 words that have been constant over time and are expected regardless of the generation. I am personally as glad that those have lasted the test of time.

As for writing thank you notes, it was my mother's most emphatic expectation. You get birthday gifts, write a thank you note. Graduation cards with cash, write a thank you note. The interesting caveat was that the present or money could not be used until the thank you note was mailed. I continued that expectation with my kids, but I have seen a morph in the delivery. Now, as adults, in place of the mailed thank you card, it appears that an acceptable action is a text message saying thank you. Hmmm, haven't been able to get my head around that as being appropriate etiquette...yet. When discussing it with my adult kids, they see a thank you phone call or text as a serious and heartfelt way to say thank you.

Kindness and politeness are not overrated at all. They are underused. So, as grandparents, what are we doing to reinforce social etiquette? Step one, for sure, is talking to the parents to be sure you are not undermining their family etiquette focus. Step two is to share your reasons why you would like the old-fashioned mailed thank you card, or opening a door for someone, or that first fork. Whatever is important to you.

Self-Image: Small Steps Make Significant Changes

Ugh! I'm so fat, I'm not very smart, I'm ugly, nobody likes me. I would like to say that these 4 self-image distracters are the only image issues that we as parents, grandparents, humans might have to deal with, but that would be far from the truth. None of them, or all of them, maybe how you personally felt at one time, or perhaps even still do.

The 4 self-esteem issues above are only the tip of the iceberg of reasons why we might feel we are not "good enough." Every person is different, every childhood experience affects every child differently, even in the same home, and everyone copes differently.

I think I can honestly say, that if asked, every one of my sisters would agree that they were loved, every sister felt safe growing up, and every sister had exposure to family and community support. I will share with you that being one of 5 siblings did not give us the same perceptions, memories, or even baggage. Regardless of how we grew up, we can still increase our self-image as an adult. This is a never-ending process.

I'm not going to spend any time writing about Maslow's hierarchy of needs, but this pyramid was built in the early 1940s, and the accepted theory of foundational basics is that if some of our initial conditions are unmet, we may be unable to progress and meet our other needs.

So, back to self-image. If we have high self-esteem, we feel liked, accepted, confident, and proud of who we are and think good things about ourselves. In essence, we believe in ourselves.

Let's take a quick personal quiz. Don't worry, you don't have to share with anyone unless you want to. So, find a piece of paper and pencil, even your computer and keyboard will do. Let's get started.

I encourage you to honestly answer these questions:

1- What do you like about yourself?

You might be surprised by how good it feels to sit down and reflect on what you like about yourself. Don't limit yourself to typical things like a friendly smile. Try listing things like being observant of the little things, volunteering at a dog shelter, or appreciating your ability to make time for others.

2. How do you cope with stress?

Everyone has stress. Think about what destresses you...a massage, quiet time without any distractions, exercise... No right or wrong answer.

3. What 3 words best describe you?

Be honest and specific. Think spiritual, work, life, family...

4. What do you want to learn more about?

This is referring to your "bucket list." It could be specific travel, learning a new sport, a language, activities. Then the second part of this question is, what is stopping you from learning it? Now, just do it.

So, enough about us. Let's talk about our grandkids.

We know that when kids feel good about themselves, they have more confidence and are willing to try more new things, and if they fail at the recent activity or make mistakes, they are more apt to successfully deal with it.

Let's help build the self-image of our grandkids. Some suggestions are:

1.   Allow them to stretch outside their comfort zone. Help them learn new things and teach them that it's ok to fail.

2.   Praise them when they truly deserve it. Kids know if you give them fake praise, which plays into low self-image. Try to focus on the good, and make sure they overhear you praising and speaking highly of them.

3.   Avoid negative criticism about actions that are different than you may take

4.   Have them list 5 things that they love about themselves before going to sleep

5.   If body image is an issue, help them find clothes that flatter their body style.

6.   Demonstrate and encourage kindness

7.   Help them find new things that are interesting to them. Look for something they may not have everyday exposure to; museums, art classes, short-road trips, activities/sports outside their typical day (curling, pickleball, board games).

8.   Just do something fun.

Making these 8 activities top of mind and creating a sustainable action plan that can be done daily or weekly will make it a habit and can go a long way toward boosting their self-image.

Think about the adults in your life. Maybe today is the day to say something positive about them. Remember, self-image can be a constant balance.

A Promise is a Promise

"A promise is a promise." A phrase that emphasizes that a promise should be kept. As a young girl, my mom taught me that keeping your promises is the backbone of any healthy relationship. When it came to arriving on time, my mom drilled into me that you should never be late at an early age. My mom was never late and usually arrived early to any event, appointment, or meeting.

I took this to heart and instilled this in all my relationships moving forward. For dates, I was always ready when my guy came to pick me up at the house. Being very aware of coming home from my dates when I promised my parents I would return. I was always on time for work at the family liquor store when I was in High School.

In college, I continued to be on time and had roommates that drove me crazy when they were late all the time. My mantra for years is that I promise to arrive on time, come hell or high water. A prevalent phrase back in the day. What baffles me today is how we got around without Waze and Google maps when traveling by car and be on time to meet up with friends and family. We would have to pull off the highway, find a payphone, insert a quarter, and somehow know their phone numbers. I guess we all had paper address books to reference, or I had a better memory back then than I do today.

As a young adult, my obligations did not hold the same weight that they will later in my life. But what I learned about promises and the importance of keeping them will affect me as I get older and grow into adulthood. Another promise I made to myself was to always make my bed and hang up my clothes before I left my dorm, apartment, or house. My mom instilled in me the concept of organization.

A true promise is made by someone who can keep it, for example, my wedding vows to my husband of almost 27 years and his vows to me on our special day. A person who can keep a promise enhances that person's character and integrity. My mom was known for being prompt and keeping her promises even at the young age of 85 when meeting her best friend at the pool every morning or playing ping pong every evening. She was the queen of her kingdom and was admired by all.

I have two daughters, now young adults, who look up to me, as I am their mother. I promise them every day to always love them, and I know they understand the idea of keeping a promise. As a family, we were always on time, and I believe this trait and commitment will continue with my grandchildren when that day comes. Me, a grandparent? I can't wait.

Please, don't be late. Promise?

Charm School: Are Manners Still Relevant?

What is Charm school, and what does it teach? Sometimes called Finishing schools, these programs focused on teaching social graces. In the 1800s, these schools were established to train young women to become polished, accomplished wives and socialites. In other words, we are preparing them for marriage.

In Chicago circa 1946, Patricia Stevens Finishing School was established as a charm and modeling school. Its charge was to indoctrinate young women on the importance of personal appearance and proper behavior. Side note, Did

You Know? That Howard Hughes hired Patricia Stevens to train their flight attendants at TWA (Transworld Airlines)?

Growing up in Chicago, I vividly remember my four older sisters attending Patricia Stevens. They had a circular suitcase adorned with flower power stickers. Although I wasn't aware of the contents, I envied their glamor lessons and fashion show catwalks.

But as I approached adolescence, perceptions of women's role in society changed. Focus on academics and professional pursuits for women, along with bra burning, became the trend. Coincidently, societal changes occurred when my sisters were off to college. So, I wasn't privileged to have a fancy charm school experience.

My oldest sister attended St. Mary's College, a women's school with a co-exchange program to Notre Dame. Mistakenly, people sometimes refer to women's colleges as finishing schools. But elite schools didn't allow women as students directly until 1971. As a chemistry major, my sister would be severely offended by such a remark regarding it as a finishing school.

And I attended an all-girls high school in the late 1970s, which also migrated to a co-ed institution in 1988. Although its mission is to impact society positively, they were considered a college prep institution, not a charm school. But looking back, our skirts were supposed to touch the ground when we knelt, clog-type shoes were considered out of uniform code, and jackets and solid-colored long sleeves shirts were required. Swearing was not an option, nor was talking back to a nun. It sounds a little like Patricia Steven's focus on "the importance of personal appearance and proper behavior."

Today, Charm schools might be scarce, but manners are still important. Since my parents, sisters, and high school gave me solid ground on manners, I was prepared to act appropriately when I became an adult. Good manners, courtesy, and etiquette are the building blocks of a healthy society.

Fast forward to my experience raising children. Instilling good manners became difficult with three rambunctious, rowdy boys. Burping, farting, and eating with your mouth open were everyday mealtime activities. Teaching the magic words "thank you" and "please" seemed to the extent of their gentile skills. Trying to keep them in their seat for more than five minutes was a constant challenge. Where are the charm schools for boys?

I did find one. It was a class like Queen City Etiquette. The boys went to a school for six weeks learning the basics of manners through the etiquette of five-star dining. So fast forward to this new era; Finishing schools aren't around, and even Queen City Etiquette has their children's classes on hold. So where does this generation learn manners?

As grandparents, we can encourage proper behavior through various activities. When grandkids visit, stage an afternoon tea. Yes, girls and boys alike enjoy teatime with pretend food and drink. My mother-in-law treated our boys to tea with a miniature China set. They were much more inclined to be on their best behavior for their grandma.

Spending time with grandparents is integral to a kid's education. Showing respect for their elders is essential to have good manners. And what better people to learn compassion from than a grandparents' wisdom and patience?

There are also printed materials and activities to teach manners. Now is your opportunity to impact your grandchild's world by opening their minds to a kinder, gentler time with good manners.

Manners: How it Can Change the World

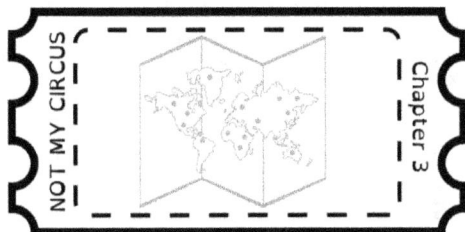

In today's age of societal turmoil, manners are more important than ever. Good manners, courtesy, and etiquette are the building blocks of a healthy society. If you want to "Change the World," begin with style and grace, not hate and disdain. Don't be a Karen.

Do you notice young kids misbehaving in public? As a grandparent, you just have to smile. You have been there with your own children's misbehavior. A perfectly well-behaved child can turn into a demon for public display of your lack of parenting skills at that moment in time. But how a parent reacts is critical to a child's development.

Is the parent ignoring the child and continuing to talk or text on the phone? Or are they trying to have a logical discussion with a toddler throwing a temper tantrum and asking them to "use their words." Either way is not the most effective at that instant, but we are bystanders. This is Not Your Circus, Not Your Monkeys.

Being a grandparent means biting your lip regarding differences in parenting styles. However, knowing the importance of manners, you can be an influence. Helping young children learn the art of proper etiquette as a grandparent will give them a foundation for success. Here are some reasons why it is important to start young:

1. Instilling Confidence – Doubt is eliminated if we know how to act in various situations. It saves us from embarrassment.

2. Making the Best First Impression – It is intimidating to meet someone for the first

time, but you are prepared with politeness, proper speech, and manner.

3. Opening Doors – When opportunity comes along, it is often the polite, well-mannered individuals who are thought of because people remember how you made them feel.

4. Cultivating Society – Consideration for others by holding the door, offering help, and saying please and thank you pays it forward because you are thinking about someone besides yourself.

5. Preventing Selfishness – Rudeness and concern for only yourself breed loneliness. It is impossible to be mindful of others and selfish simultaneously.

6. Sparking Joy – There is a deep satisfaction in helping others; it brings joy.

7. Inspiring Reciprocation – It is easy to be nice when someone is nice to you. As they say, kill them with kindness.

8. Laying the Foundation of Success – Proper etiquette brings respect. Respect leads to trust, which is the basis of every solid relationship.

9. Fostering Relationships – Who wants to be around a loud, rude, uncouth person? Manners assist in developing bonds between people.

10. Making Others Feel Appreciated – Noticing others' contributions will make them and you more confident.

Here are our recommendations if you need help with resources to influence raising well-mannered kids.

For Classes, we recommend:

Etiquette Essentials 101 for 6-11-year-olds

The British School of Excellence Kidiquette is an online course for kids aged 5-11

For Books, we recommend:

Connoisseur Kids: Etiquette, Manners, and Living Well for Parents and Their Little Ones for parents.

Do Unto Otters for 3 – 7-year-olds.

Suppose You Meet A Dinosaur for 3 – 6-year-olds

Teach Your Dragon Manners for 4 – 8-year-olds.

Margaret Wise Brown's Manners for 3 – 5-year-olds.

There are also printed materials and activities to teach manners. If you are looking for more resources, follow us at cjcorki.com. Now is your opportunity to "Change the World" by instilling good manners in your children and grandchildren.

Plates of All Shapes

Let's talk about manners!

With summer finally here, temperatures start to heat up, and we begin wearing shorts and flip-flops again. Additionally, disposable cups, plates, and other easily disposable paraphernalia become the norm. This single action of paper product usage has single-handedly ended manners as we know it!

Now that I have your attention let's spend a minute discussing our dining experiences.

Let's first start with a question. Do you believe that using fine China daily elevates your dining experience and teaches us to be more mindful of our table manners?

Growing up, the answer for us would have been an emphatic "no." Not only because we didn't have fine China dishes, but meals were a means to an end, a full tummy. Now that doesn't mean we were without manners. We still learned not to put our elbows on the table, never to talk with our mouths full, and we even knew what side the fork, spoon, and knife belonged to.

Every family is unique, so as a grandparent, you may discover that how you raised your child differs significantly from your kid's choice of dining etiquette rules for your grandkids.

As an adult, I was shocked to find out that my cousins, who only live a few miles from me, had such a different dining experience compared to mine.

Their household used fine China instead of Melmac plates for all meals regardless of special or regular dining occasions. Not only were plated breakable and hand-washed every day, but the fancy glassware and complete silverware were laid out, including more than the three utensils of my youth. In addition, "dressing for dinner" was an expectation.

Did I feel like I missed an opportunity? Nope. We went to their house every Thanksgiving and had that "experience." Pretty dresses, linen napkins, and the fear of breaking their fine China is the memory I have. If there was a manners lesson served up, I missed it.

As an adult, I ultimately learned to eat seamlessly with all the fine dinnerware and to "dress up" appropriately. Whenever I have that opportunity, I think of my aunt and her focus on using proper utensils, setting the table just right, and everything in between. I still worry I might break something.

Dining etiquette choices...not necessarily right, just right for them.

Don't fret if formal dining seems daunting during summer! Even simpler paper plate etiquette will show good manners if used along with polite phrases such as please and thank you, placing a napkin on a lap, and not talking with their mouth full. Every meal gives us an opportunity to demonstrate proper dining etiquette and consideration towards those present, regardless of whether we use fancy dinnerware or not.

Let's make every meal a great opportunity to practice manners and show respect to those around us...with or without fine China.

In case you didn't know, Melmac refers to a type of dinnerware produced from Melamine resin, an environmentally friendly plastic material that was trendy during the latter part of the 1960s.

FUN THINGS TO DO

Talk:

Talk about leading by example and consistently reinforce these values in everything they do. Learning proper etiquette at a young age cultivates respect, empathy, and social skills, forming a strong foundation for positive interactions, personal growth, and future success in relationships and society.

Recommend to Read:

- How Do Dinosaurs Eat Their Food? by Jane Yole

- Everyday Graces: A Child's Book of Good Manners by Karen Santorum

- Excuse Me: A Little Book of Manners by Karen Katz

Questions to Ask:

Why is it important to share toys and take turns with friends?

Can you think of a time when you were kind to someone? How did it make you and the other person feel?

How do you feel when someone says "please" and "thank you" to you?

CORE VALUE: GRACE

Teaching kids good manners is teaching them kindness, consideration and courtesy.

Stories:

Books:

Questions Asked:

4

Legacy Tech: Yesterday's Wonders, Today's Nostalgia

Getting information off the Internet is like taking a drink from a fire hydrant.
Mitch Kapor

117

Introduction

From a grandparent's perspective, technology has transformed the world in ways we couldn't comprehend when we were children. It is awe-inspiring and overwhelming to witness the rapid advancements that have become an integral part of our daily lives. While I may embrace new technology challenges, I appreciate that many grandparents might struggle. We sometimes long for the simplicity of yesteryears, where face-to-face conversations and handwritten letters carried a profound sense of warmth and intimacy. Nonetheless, we should recognize technology's immense opportunities, empowering younger generations to learn, create, and explore like never before. Let your grandchildren take the lead to show you the nuances of their world of technology to build even stronger bonds with the rising generation.

Growing Up with Big, Beige, and Boring Technology

NOT MY CIRCUS

Chapter 4

"It is painful to watch Boomers use technology," my 30-something son told me as I tried to reset the internet. Although I think I am pretty tech-savvy, I grew up with Big, Beige, and Boring technology. He, on the other hand, was raised with high-tech gadgets. What earliest technology do you remember? How old were you? Was it boring or fun?

The first personal computer I remember using in the 1980s was definitely big, beige, and boring. The operating system it used was MS-DOS which used the language called BASIC (Beginners' All-purpose Symbolic Instruction Code). It was a huge advancement for me since I was programming in FORTRAN on a mainframe that accepted keypunch cards. Did I say I was old?

Fast forward to 1985, when Microsoft's Windows was released. Having just graduated from Georgia Tech, where I spent hours in a computer lab, I started my new job using an IBM Computer with windows. Talk about mind-blowing. No longer did I need all the coding I used in college. Just clicking on an icon did an enormous amount of pre-programmed work.

However, these computers were extremely slow, taking all day to run macros. And what would be considered a portable computer weighed 20 pounds! Yes, still big, beige, and boring. They used floppy discs, which didn't have a lot of storage capacity. In 1990 CD-ROMs were then introduced. By then, I was working in Boston using computers that needed to store a lot of data. This new technology was revolutionary. I remember clearly my colleague introducing me to this new way to store data. I quickly adopted its use to help with my work efficiency.

My work as a management consultant needed the latest technology. We were using Apple's Macintosh and began to transition from Lotus 1-2-3 spreadsheets to Excel. Our presentations were done in PowerPoint in the late 80s and early 90s. But we still had to FedEx presentations since this was the pre-internet era.

Working in the downtown Boston office, jetting all over the country, and working with senior executives gave me great exposure to the newest technologies. However, all my technology applications were for work. Shortly after our first son was born, when I was a stay-at-home mom, I still tried to keep up with technology. We had our own computer, just one, but how many did you need? I used it to track finances with QuickBooks and Word for writing. It was the first time outside of the work environment that we used technology.

Many from the younger generation typically assume that Baby Boomers are stuck in their old-school, traditional ways and want nothing to do with any modern features in technology. But we were early adopters of all kinds of technology.

My husband had a cell phone for work that was mounted in his car. I had a cordless landline too. We got a big screen TV which had rear projection. It even had a VHS so the kids could watch movies. All these things were Big, Beige, and Boring still. It isn't that our generation doesn't like technology; it is used for functionality. It wasn't until Apple revolutionized design that it changed the world of technology.

Distinctive design—clean, friendly, and fun—would become the hallmark of Apple products under Steve Jobs. He had the vision for a friendly computer, a very forward-thinking view. No longer is a computer just about function, but about having fun. Introducing the distinct differences between young vs. older users.

Youngsters typically use their forms of technology to "pass the time" and use social media platforms to interact with people. Older people primarily use technology for more functional and business purposes to connect with people and learn how to market their companies. So how do you bridge the technology gap?

Millennials and Gen Z grandchildren are the natives of technology. They can use their expertise to help grandparents become more technologically familiar and fluent in the latest "fun" technology. This would allow everyone to understand and use technology efficiently for both personal and career life.

As baby boomers, if you are heading into retirement age, it would be advantageous to learn to use technology outside of the workplace. Not just for functional use but to enjoy life. What lessons would you like to learn from your grandchild? They would be happy to help. Break out of the Big, Beige, and Boring world and trade in your flip phone for one that is fun. Consider one with bling, a selfie stick, or other gadgets.

Tech-Savvy Grandkids at Your Service: Unlocking the Digital World of Communication Together!

NOT MY CIRCUS

Chapter 4

As the Greatest Generation member, my mom was technologically advanced, especially for her age. She was a wiz with spreadsheets. She created manual spreadsheets before technology caught up to her. She eagerly took to social media, even posting her version of a selfie to share with family and friends. Computer, Smart Phone, iPad, yep, she used them all. But she gladly leaned on her children and grandchildren for technology questions.

Tapping into the grandchild resource is an excellent option for this rising generation of grandparents. Don't be embarrassed, Baby Boomers. You can save a lot of frustration, money, and time by asking grandkids.

Our oldest son is currently in a technology role as his profession. When he was younger, he locked my computer screen to look like it was melting subsequently. Since it was password protected, I had to call the middle school to ask him for the password to unlock my screen. Yes, a fifth grader could lock me out of my computer. A year later, he begged to be on his Xbox to play other gamers online with people he didn't know. As a protective parent, I refused to allow it. As a result, he hacked into the system. He could play without parental approval and oversight and for free. Yes, Xbox eventually shut him down and banded him for a period. However, I was unaware of the breach until he became an adult.

My point is that children and grandchildren are outpacing us with technology by leaps and bounds. They grew up with the internet and thrived on keeping up with the latest gadgets. Video games were part of their childhood.

But why fight it? Early on, I knew I could never put a tracker on my teenage boys. They would hack it and put it on the dog or something else obscure for me to follow. However, they expected to report every night via text if they changed their location or when they were coming home. They were using technology in my realm of comfort.

As grandparents, technology isn't a resource for curfew; it is a great bonding tool. My mom took a texting class in her 80s because she wanted to learn to communicate with her grandchildren. Finding a communication avenue to keep in touch is an important step.

I have learned that there are better tools to communicate than email. Yes, they will eventually get the email, but if it is time sensitive, know there won't be a quick response. A phone call? No, that generally is not the best way to communicate since they might be in the middle of something. Unless there is an emergency, a phone call without a heads-up via text is not the best option. Text, Text, Text is the best way to get their attention.

As a family, we have a group text. We keep each other updated on events that happen and want to share. Pictures, emojis, etc., are a great way to interact with children and grandchildren. Hence the reason my mom wanted to learn how to text. Granted, Smartphones made it more accessible. I don't think I could text on a flip phone.

My sisters and the extended family also use group texts to keep in touch. My mom used email to communicate with the family daily. In the morning, she would email the temperatures of where each of her daughters, then her saying, Love, Hugs, Blessings (LHB) every night. As the next generation, we converted the emails to group text: same purpose, but different technology.

How will you bond with your grandchildren? Are you using the postal service to mail them letters? That is great, but Millennials aren't in the habit of relying on mail to communicate. And if you write in cursive, they probably cannot read it. Maybe phone calls are your thing. However, don't expect them to pick up. An unannounced call is usually only used for emergencies. Texting, yes, learn to text. But how will we communicate with the next generation, who knows?

Let them take the lead if you want to bond with your grandchildren. Ask them how they would like to keep in touch. Is Facetime preferred to a phone call, or is it Zoom? Should it be scheduled? Most likely, yes, but ask.

As the rising generation outpaces the prior one in technology, don't fight change. Embrace the latest and greatest out there, asking for help along the way.

A Grandmother's Epiphany:
Can I find Joy Off the Grid?

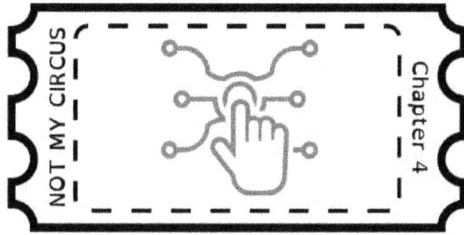

What were the longest 48 hours in YOUR Life?
A mere 2,880 minutes. 172,800 seconds. How
hard could it be to live through something like
that?

I have always been fascinated by time my entire
existence on this earth. The old film of the 1960s,
The Time Machine with Yvette Mimieux, takes a
scientist into the future to find a Utopian society.
Or maybe you remember, Back to the Future,
where they find out you never really know what
your parents were like when they were our age.

With a bit of research, I found Einstein's and Stephen Hawking's thoughts about time travel too!

Even with my infatuation with time and time travel, I recently experienced a 48-hour journey into h*ll. Yep, time, as I knew it, was gone.

Worse than standing still, the hours, minutes, and seconds seemed to be moving at a snail's pace, with no end in sight. No one around me could see the minutes freezing or the night shadows playing tricks as I wonder if I was in an alternate universe, my personal Twilight Zone.

My ability to gather information stopped and the connection to the outside world I came to rely on was lost. I was adrift and alone in a vast array of humanity. I was on this journey alone.

Did I wish these 48 hours had happened to me? No, it was thrust upon me, and I was unprepared for this.

Of course, I should have been. I remember a time when you needed to gather information, you went to the library building eight blocks away. I grew up talking across the fence with neighbors to have the human connection we all require, and yes even learned to sit in a small group and entertain ourselves by singing into candlesticks or playing in the cubby hole.

Today, in the world of connecting, my connection was lost. Literally. I had no Internet.

Some of you may be shocked that this should have such a devastating effect on me, but I kid you not. I now truly understand what it would be like if our grandkids were not connected. I have walked in their shoes!

If you have been following our blogs and posts, you know that we have been a big proponent of screen-free days and participating in activities where the only equipment required is our brain and imagination. That, however, has been shattered. These 48 hours taught me one important lesson. Balance, not absolutes, is the key.

Let me take you on a trip down memory lane. After all, it was only 32* years ago that the mainstream world was internet free.

Why is this important? Because 32 years ago, our grandkids weren't around, and maybe not even our kids. The world that we spend so much time reminiscing about or reminding them of better times is long gone. The phrases we have probably used with them, include, "when I was a kid..." or "back in the day...." This is as out of date as talking to them about life for kids in ancient Egypt.

I am not saying to throw away our desire to connect with people and nature, but I am saying that some good has come out of change. Change is constant, and blending the old, AND the new will make for a better future.

Let's have some fun with this situation. Pose questions and activities to try for yourself or with your grandkids. Some that are front of mind include:

- What would I do if I don't have connectivity for 48 hours?
- How would you gather information?
- Which friends would you get together with face-to-face? What would you do?
- What would you do differently if you didn't have Internet 1 day a week...forever?

Now go and try it.

Life without technology? I know what you are thinking...heresy!

It isn't easy to imagine living without the technology we know and love. We owe technology for our modern and comfortable way of life in our everyday interactions. You are probably asking yourself if there was no technology, do you need to go back and find an old-fashioned alarm clock? Waking up can suddenly become a chore. Right? How would I wake up? Picture this—no Alexa or smartphone to provide my snooze. The slow, but rising sound of the music as time allows me to flutter my eyes open slowly. My window shades are timed to go up to bring in the morning light, and finally, my drop-dead alarm ring is no longer available. Ugh!

Or what about the time change? We just went through the change to daylight saving time. Do you remember just a short week away when we spring forward? It used to be easy. Now, without technology, every appliance, TV, and automobile no longer seamlessly and mysteriously move to the correct time. Oh no...Who is going to handle that for you?

In fact, right from dawn to dusk, technology is with us. I know we use our smartphone to call a friend, find out the latest world event, or maybe even view our 'ring' doorbell, to name just a few. We are enjoying the benefits of information technology at its finest. Yes, technology is my friend and yours. We want to, no, need to, treat technology with respect, awe, and reverence as we now have information at our fingertips.

Please consider putting aside your reliance on technology for a day, or maybe a weekend, and enjoy the no-tech world of nature at its finest.

Spring is about to begin. The weather will be fluid, regardless of where in the country you live. Think about it. You don't need to check the weather app to see what the weather holds in store for you this weekend. Trust me, look out the window, open the door, and feel the air... you'll know.

Great, we are off to a strong start. Next, rally the grandkids. These activities also work virtually, so give them a little heads up on technology-free weekends and set them up for some fantastic memories.

So, what do you "do" with them? In the resources section of our website (cjcorki.com), we have captured some great ideas that engage the senses, imagination, and wonder, but here are the top three things to do that are tech-free.

#1 – Take a nature scavenger hunt. There are animals, nature, and beauty that only happen in the spring, right in front of us. See a caterpillar crawling on a nearby branch. Days from now, it will become a cocoon and then, if by magic, become a butterfly. Take a scavenger hunt and find all the joys of spring. We have provided a scavenger hunt card for your use, but feel free to use your imagination and find things that may only be found in your city, town, or street.

#2- Ride a bike. Two-wheel, Four-wheel, training wheel, it doesn't matter. Young and old alike can enjoy the wind in our faces, helmets on our heads, air in our tires, and maybe a basket packed for an impromptu picnic. Now find a patch of grass, and perhaps even an ant or two will show up and can be checked off on your scavenger hunt.

#3- Pull out the chalk. The sidewalks have been cleaned by nature and are ready for the budding artist to create whatever our imagination provides—Yellow, pink, and green flowers, kids in shorts and smiles, or maybe even a hopscotch game. Whatever the imagination offers, a little chalk can capture it.

I know it's easier said than done, but with a positive attitude, a commitment to be "tech-free," and an enthusiastic challenge to your grandkids, you might be pleasantly surprised with the results—

Distance Doesn't Matter: Discover the World with Your Grandkids Through Virtual Travel

Let's start tripping...

Near or far, we've got a few exciting ways for grandparents and grandkids to connect, learn, and have a blast together using the power of modern technology. Read on if you want to make lasting memories and build a strong bond, no matter the distance. So, put on your digital thinking caps, and let's embark on an incredible journey together!

Today we will talk about virtual travel and a few tips and tricks.

As my dad used to say, "The world is yours. Go out and get it." We see our grandkids free time less free, with scheduled dance classes, soccer, and swimming lessons, to name a few. So, let's not fight them; let's join them. Let's take you and your grandkids on virtual trips to various parts of the world using technology. From exploring ancient ruins in Greece to a wildlife safari in Africa, each adventure can be filled with fascinating facts, engaging quizzes, and interactive activities.

Virtual travel offers a range of opportunities, such as exploring places from the comfort of your home, learning about new cultures, and engaging in interactive activities.

How do we accomplish this? Well, a great starting place is your personal nationality. Where did you come from? No, this isn't about the birds and the bees, but rather your family story. My sisters and I are of Polish descent. Even though we are 3rd generation Americans, the tie to the experiences, stories, and family across the pond is strong. What's yours?

Using virtual travel can be an end in and of itself, or it can be a prequel to an actual family trip where you are ultimately physically present. Think about different traditions, customs, and lifestyles. Are there important museums and historical sites? There is a rich history of humankind to be shared.

What about taking them on a culinary journey? Make a traditional dish. I would start with Czarnina (duck blood soup), a Polish delicacy. After they get past the name, they can learn about the ingredients you used, when someone might make this, and an added benefit of making something so unusual would become a great story to share and gross-out friends.

Depending on the age of the grandkids, have them become a videographer or travel journalists writing (or drawing) stories about the new virtual location.

Virtual travel is a game-changer for enhancing your relationships. It offers several benefits, such as accessibility, affordability, and convenience. Virtual travel allows travelers to explore previously inaccessible destinations because of time or cost and learn about new cultures. It provides a glimmer of hope and an opportunity to experience the world from the comfort of our homes. Even though my dad never thought about the virtual side of his statement, it is still true, "The world IS yours, go out and get it."

We hope we have sparked some ideas. We are dedicated to helping you nurture that special connection between grandparents and grandkids in the digital age. By embracing technology, we can break barriers, have fun, and create lasting memories together. So, let's embark on this exciting journey of exploration, creativity, and togetherness.

Disclaimer: Remember that your and your grandkids' safety and privacy are important, so let's make sure we monitor their online activities and use appropriate security measures.

Alexa, Are You My Grandmother?

As modern grandmas, we answer to a variety of names. Our young grandchildren might affectionately call us Mimi, Gaga, Nana, or even Grammy. But getting called "Alexa" or "Siri" might make you pause. Those three-year-olds consistently asking "Why?" typically get a patient and accurate response from Grandma, while frazzled parents might say, go ask Alexa. Although using technology can be a lifesaver, overuse of technology can mask the early signs of dyslexia.

Virtual assistants, including Amazon's Alexa, are designed to provide voice-activated assistance and perform tasks based on voice commands.

They can read text aloud and help with specific tasks like setting reminders or answering questions.

Computer Generated voices started in the 1960s. However, in the 1980s, some of my classmates at Georgia Tech made tremendous milestone advances with the first commercially successful text-to-speech systems. I remember the Atlanta airport train system initially having a robotic male voice. It quickly was changed to a female voice to sound more welcoming. Progress!

Fast forward to the 2000s when our son used Dragon/Naturally Speaking to record papers for school. He was diagnosed with dyslexia and dysgraphia in 4th grade. Since writing things down was a challenge, it was considered an excellent tool to resolve the homework dilemma. Unfortunately, technology still wasn't that advanced, and he could never train it with his young voice.

But now, there are numerous advanced software tools for dyslexic and non-dyslexic children alike. Alexa, Siri, and Google Assistant are just a few popular ones that are used for information daily. "How do you spell banana?" "How do you say A-R-M-A-D-I-L-O?" "What is 5 + 9?" Using these tools like this can also cover a child's underlying learning issues.

Is your grandkid using these tools to help them with homework? One sign is that they complete their assignment quickly and without too much struggle but fail their in-school tests. Or are they constantly asking Alexa how to pronounce a word, and it might be the same word over again? These tools can be great, but if they haven't been diagnosed yet with a learning style difference, it could mask an early diagnosis.

As a parent or grandparent, what can you do? Become familiar with the early signs of dyslexia. You can identify some subtle signs as early as three years old. Turn off Alexa if your child seems too dependent on it. Check with teachers if they are in school and ask them what they observe. Be proactive and insist on formal testing if deemed necessary.

But technology such as Alexa can be used successfully as a tool for learning. It is an excellent resource for information. Much better than the encyclopedias we have in our day. Use it for time management by setting timers to monitor studying and reminders for upcoming assignments and tests. It can be used as an audiobook, which was a massive help in getting my kids through reading assignments. If they follow along with an actual book, it will help their reading proficiency and help with words they have never seen before. Alexa can also provide study break reminders and music to help your children relax.

So, grandparents embrace technology as valuable devices to assist with learning, not hinder it. Be aware of its masking symptoms of dyslexia by learning more about the early signs. And be flattered that you are being called Alexa; you have the wisdom of ages and the patience of gods.

"Like the gods, patience carves masterpieces from the stone of time." Chat GPT

This quote was created with Artificial Intelligence (AI), a technology discussion for another day.

FUN THINGS TO DO

Talk:

Share with them how technology has changed over the years. Talk about the devices and gadgets you used when you were their age and compare them to the technologies they have today. Discuss how technology has transformed various aspects of life, such as communication, entertainment, and education.

Recommend to Read:

- Once Upon a Time... Online: Happily Ever After Is Only a Click Away! - David Bedford

- Goodnight iPad: a Parody for the next generation Ann Droyd

- Dot. - Randi Zuckerberg

Questions to Ask:

What is your favorite thing to do with technology?

Can you tell me about a game or app you enjoy playing?

Can you name some electronic devices you know?

CORE VALUE:
CONNECTION

Learning and using technology to deepen the bond between grandparents and grandchildren in a user-friendly way.

Stories:

Books:

Questions Asked:

5

When Words are Hard: Early Signs of Learning Differences

You can take this obstacle [dyslexia] and make it a reason to have a big heart. It takes obstacles to learn, grow, be better.
Orlando Bloom

Introduction

Early identification of learning differences is crucial for providing timely interventions, support, and accommodations that address the specific learning needs of children with dyslexia. By promoting dyslexia awareness, we empower parents and grandparents to be advocates for their children to develop their literacy skills, emotional well-being, and self-confidence.

Children as early as three years old can be identified if parents and grandparents know the signs. Waiting for them to start school and struggle will inhibit their ability to catch up with their classmate in the long term. Be a grandparent to promote dyslexia awareness by becoming informed.

Early Identification of Dyslexia

Did you know that one in five children are Dyslexic? Dyslexia is more than reversing letters. It is a learning difference. The medical profession actually can see the differences in brain activity between non-dyslexic and dyslexic brains. Children experience letters jumping around the page when they read. However, it is considered an invisible disability. What children see comes out in other ways, such as hyperactivity, depression, or disruptive behavior. Parents and teachers want their children to succeed but are helpless when it comes to solutions.

Let's start with the early signs. In preschool, a child would have a hard time with rhymes. If you ask your child: mat, bat, cat, what word comes next? Our youngest dyslexic son responded with dog. Obviously, dog does not rhyme, but the last word he heard was cat, a house pet. His association was with other house pets, a dog. Our oldest son, who is also Dyslexic, did not have this issue but was challenged when you asked the question a different way: bat, change the "a" to a "u," and what would the word be? He wouldn't say anything. He was just confused. The word "but" had no meaning to him. It wasn't a picture he could see in his mind.

Another early sign is late speech development. Late speech could be a sign of many things but is very common with people with dyslexia. Our oldest son talked at the average rate, so we didn't have a concern. Our middle son was an early talker, so it was surprising when our youngest didn't speak until after his second birthday. He could tell you what he wanted with action, but not with words. His frustration came out with the terrible two tantrums when he couldn't be understood. Yes, terrible twos are challenging, but it is a red flag when they aren't speaking, only grunting.

Many dyslexic preschoolers call things by the wrong name or cannot come up with familiar names for objects. Our youngest son had many examples of naming errors. He once called kayaking "cadillacing" since his grandparents had both a kayak and a Cadillac. He also vividly remembers not being able to come up with the word basketball. He explained that he wanted the type of ball that you throw into a hoop.

A sure sign of dyslexia is trouble with spelling at any age. Our oldest could get 100% on a spelling test because he memorized the words in first grade. However, he could not spell the exact words in a sentence that same day. The spelling word list was just that, a list. The actual meaning of the word, a picture, was something more challenging. He had to visualize the image, decipher the sounds, form the letters, and physically write it down. It was too much for a little dyslexic first-grader to handle. Our youngest son had weird concoctions for his spelling words. The more he studied, the worse his words would be spelled. I never did figure out his rationale, but I was told they see words as shapes. The picture of how the word looked made sense to him.

As school progressed, things became more difficult. I volunteered numerous times in the classroom when our children were young. An interesting challenge included copying anything from the board. The teacher would generally give up and give our son whatever she was putting on the projector. Assignments written on the board made it a double whammy since he never could write down his assignments, thus missing homework.

Sounding out words is difficult for people with dyslexia. I remember going on a college visit with our boys. Our oldest son came across a word he never saw before, armadillo. He tried hard to sound it out, arm-ad-illo, he said. I said, you mean ar-ma-dil-lo? Even though he butchered the word, his younger brother cheered. "Yay, you sounded it out." Yes, our son was 18 years old at the time. Dyslexia is not something you outgrow.

When children are confused by books and their stories, it is a symptom of dyslexia. We had our son tested at the "All Kinds of Minds" institute (which has changed over the years). I was able to observe the testing remotely. I was fascinated when our son read a non-fiction book. His recall of the story was perfect. But when he read fiction, and the story implied various meanings, he was lost at recalling what he just read. Fascinating.

Confusing letters are typically what people think of people with dyslexia. But transposing a "b" and a "d" is just the tip of the iceberg. I was always confused that our youngest son didn't see the correlation between an "E" and an "e." They look nothing alike, so having one capital letter and another small didn't mean anything to him. He is now 28 years old and still randomly will write a capital E in the middle of a word.

Early on, sight words were a challenge for our boys. Where and were, their and there were impossible to differentiate. They could not form a picture in their mind about what the words meant and why there were different spellings. A solution was a multi-sensory experience such as blowing on their arm. "Where" had a breath while "were" did not. For there, we would point to "there" as a place to go, and "their" we would point to a person.

Not understanding idioms is a less obvious sign since it is usually revealed by not understanding the conversation. We don't realize how often we use idioms in everyday conversation. "Don't let the cat out of the bag." "It's a piece of cake." "You can't judge a book by its cover." "Rain or Shine" These are all very common sayings, but it is common for a dyslexic child to be confused and not speak up. However, our son became very concerned when an invitation to a birthday party was on rain or shine. He adamantly wanted me to call the host to make sure the party was still on. I kept insisting it was on rain or shine. He finally said, "Mom, I get the rain part, but I don't understand the shine part."

Although none of our boys have dyscalculia, defined as a learning difficulty that affects an individual's ability to do basic arithmetic such as addition, subtraction, multiplication, and division, we did have some math issues. In 5th grade, our youngest son came home saying he was confused in math class. He said the teacher kept asking what the "some" is of a particular math problem. I explained that she was referring to a different word, "sum," not some. When I said "sum" means to add, he felt relieved. Now, he understood the homework assignment.

If you see any of these signs in your young children, don't hesitate to see your school administrators have your child tested. Knowledge is your child's superpower.

Words are Hard:
How Do Children Cope?

The English language, by most standards, is challenging to learn. Spelling is weird. Did you know that only English-speaking countries have "spelling bees?" Why, you ask? Because in other languages, spelling is more predictable. But spelling is about writing; language is about speaking. English features grammatical rules that are often broken, an alphabet that can confuse people who are used to a character-based system, and spelling and pronunciation irregularities that confuse even native speakers. So how do the little ones learn to speak?

In the beginning, there are most likely mistakes. Many young kids say adorable things to describe something they heard incorrectly or cannot remember. Some memorable ones include "spread cheese" instead of shredded cheese or "boo-boo bus" instead of an ambulance. Some mispronunciations are embarrassing, like saying "f**k" instead of fork or truck. Or "titty" instead of kitty. Or maybe a difficult-to-pronounce word, like mayonnaise, comes out as band-aids, something they are more familiar with seeing.

Our youngest son was a late talker. He would grunt and point to what he wanted. Since he was the youngest of three active boys, an argument could be made that his brothers were talking for him, so he did not need to speak. It wasn't that he didn't understand; he didn't form the words. But his frustration revealed itself in tantrums. We sought medical advice, which resulted in speech therapy. Problem solved, or so I thought.

Learning to annunciate words is one thing; retrieving a word from memory is another. Most toddlers outgrow the mispronunciations, although some parents continue with the adorable mistakes. Once children are in elementary school, they are expected to correctly know sight words, gradually grasping more difficult words through phonetics. Coming up with the word from memory can be more challenging.

Our son would describe the word he couldn't retrieve. It would be a circular discussion about something as simple as a blister, turning it into a long dialog on "that thing that pusses and hurts and is on my foot from my shoe being tight." Or a more recent one, "the cake topping," instead of recalling the word frosting. I would joke as we would seemingly be playing a game of charades, "sounds like?"

To describe the difficulty in retrieving words, think of a deck of cards nicely organized in the brain where someone can retrieve a card at will. Other children have their cards, not in a neat deck but scattered randomly, making them more challenging to recall.

However, even organized words are still hard, leaving some children dazed and confused.

English has many words that mean two different things, which are homophones. Common ones include which/witch, here/hear, buy/by, and to/too/two. Or they can be longer words like "monarch." In our son's eighth-grade history class, the teacher asked what a monarch is; his response was a butterfly. Yes, homophones can be particularly confusing.

Teachers often say that late talking, misspeaking, poor recall, or word confusion is something a child grows out of doing. I would be skeptical. Did you know that 30% of late talkers don't outgrow their delay and will need intervention? And one in twelve children between the ages of 3-17 with early misspeaking has a communication disorder? And one in five children are Dyslexic?

Although some children with these issues may have no specific learning challenges, the odds are against them. Of course, there may be other factors affecting these language issues. In our case for late talking, our son's tonsils were too large for him to speak. Or a hearing issue may be causing children to understand what an adult is annunciating, causing misspeak. But as a parent and eventual grandparents, bringing awareness to the potential issues and their early signs is key to success in school.

How Can Anyone Fail Kindergarten?

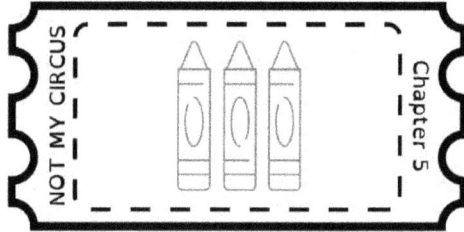

When was the first time you failed? Was it an easy fix, or did you need intervention??

As "they" say, learning begins at birth. But I will tell you that my education moved at warp speed since I was a close second to my older sister, who had a mere 11 months on me.

We made the most of our early learning moments, but they were as different as night and day. I had a fragile beginning as I followed behind someone who could quickly comprehend even the vaguest concepts, had the agility of a ninja, and the mental prowess that challenged her peers...and me. Don't feel too bad for me. After all, I, too, had honed a few skills of my own. I could read a room like nobody's business. I was the peacemaker and the middle child for the first 6 years of my life. Not necessarily skills to set me up in the academic realm but societally appropriate.

You might think this is about sibling dynamics and how it influences our personal success, but instead, this is about failing. Let's define "fail." Merriam-Webster says failing is "to be unsuccessful, to fall short, to miss performing the expected behavior."

The good news is that everyone has failed and will fail again. We sometimes forget that all successful people have failed, but they did not stop after their failures. The better news is that I am following in the footsteps of great people who have failed. I, too found a way to survive.

As we start packing the backpacks and lunchboxes, it felt appropriate to talk about our early academic years. Let's get back to kindergarten. Before starting school, my parents worked on the fundamentals: can I identify letters, hold a crayon correctly, and successfully go to the bathroom by myself? Check, check and check.

Of course, my advanced skills included using scissors correctly and I even knew not to run with them, a feat that not everyone has mastered. I was a superstar at listening without interrupting and playing appropriately with others. Superstar check.

Other than the abilities above, there was never any. Montessori learning, STEM techniques, or identifying learning challenges as part of parental thought.

I didn't know I had learning difficulties. Instead, I often heard how quick, how bright and how my older sister was going to be a doctor, so I personally compared myself to my more brilliant older sibling. I felt dumb in comparison. It was never said to me, and she never thought it, but perception is reality, and that was my reality at the early age of 4.

I observed our differences and wanted to be "smart" like her, but the letters were always jumbled, and I didn't know why. Did you know that 1 in 5 people have dyslexia?

Research has shown that calling things by the wrong name is one of the many signs. I couldn't figure out why I had to go through the sister's lists... ro, car, mar, char, mad before finally landing on the correct name of the person I was referring to. Still, to this day, I know which sister I am talking to but must go through the library of words before I land on the right one.

Did you know that 35% of people with dyslexia don't graduate from high school or that almost 70% of juvenile delinquents have dyslexia? Of course, low self-esteem and depression are unintended consequences. Struggling in Kindergarten is a red flag that can't be ignored.

Nowadays, learning is not just "one size fits all." There is intervention and help. Parents can request schools conduct an evaluation of their child. Since you don't grow out of dyslexia, discussions with teachers and family are a constant and an essential role as parents.

As grandparents, what can you do? Read, read, and read some more to your grandkids. If you notice some signs of dyslexia, work with your adult kids on the action you can take to reinforce the superpower they possess. Never focus on how academically different they are; tell them they are not dumb because they don't get it. Remember, they will "get it," just another way. One size doesn't fit all. Every child has their own set of strengths and weaknesses.

Also, find books that are written in an open dyslexic font. At CJ Corki Publishing, we are so passionate about enhancing the learning that every book we write uses this font choice. Remember, you never grow out of being dyslexic, so dyslexic adults find it useful too.

Being ready for kindergarten means that we now know not only to provide pre-school training in the fundamentals but know their strengths and weaknesses of our little tykes and partner with the school to bring out their best.

Remember, "the ones who are crazy enough to think that they can change the world are the ones who do," as profoundly stated by a fellow dyslexic, Steve Jobs.

We'd love to know how you handle learning differences in your world.

Your Child/Grandchild is Dyslexic: What Next?

NOT MY CIRCUS

Chapter 5

As a parent, you might have identified signs of dyslexia in your child. You may have a family member with dyslexia (dyslexia runs in families). Or they are just struggling in school, and you know something is just not right. If you approach your school, they might say your child is at an acceptable reading level for their grade or a regular part of development. The school told me that my youngest was a delayed reader since I must not read him at home. When I protested, saying we read daily, they asked if I displayed good reading habits in front of him. When I said no, I didn't have time to relax and read in front of them; I said I read when they are in bed. They proceeded to blame me for his poor reading. We have said this before that 1 in 5 children have dyslexia, but 1 in 100 teachers understand or are trained on the signs? Don't accept the pushback from the school. You know your child better than anyone. The question, however, is what is next?

It starts with a complete evaluation. The school psychologist can perform the assessment. If the school administration balks about it, know your rights. Put the request in writing and insist on the need to take these steps. My oldest son was in fourth grade when I finally put my foot down. They tested my child, but the report came back saying he is gifted based on his IQ but performing two grade levels below in reading. The public school said that was acceptable. I, in turn, went to an outside psychologist to get another evaluation. The report came back stating he has dyslexia, dysgraphia, and ADHD (attention deficit hyperactivity disorder). Our son, who was suffering from depression, was relieved that he now knew the issue and we could develop a plan.

The first step is to find a suitable school environment for teaching and learning. The psychologist's recommendation to us was to home-school him. Unfortunately, that would not be an option. I do not have the patience or skills to be a good teacher based on how I tried to help him with homework over the years. We did pull our children out of public school and found a private school with a class size of 18 or less. Just having a small class can make a difference. This was a painful process to evaluate the schools. We looked at parochial schools, gifted schools, dyslexic-specific schools, and even sports schools. We landed on a private school that fits all three of our children's needs. It focused on ALL learning styles, not just dyslexic or gifted. I recommend you come up with a list of requirements before venturing into shopping for a school. Examples of conditions: dyslexia awareness, learning differences, location, family impact (both financial and time). My most important requirement was to have a school to accommodate the needs of all my children.

What would be included in accommodations for a dyslexic student? Audiobooks are a great resource. You can get just about anything on Recordings for the Blind and Print Disabled. But now, Audible has a good amount of quality books for everyone's reading/listening pleasure. Our boys listened to the books and followed along with the print. This allowed them to understand words they had never seen before and get through long reading assignments with ease.

Use technology as much as possible and insist on it in the classroom. Things have come a long way in technology since our boys were young. Voice to text was at its beginning stages. Now everyone is using Alexa to get information. Voice recognition software has dramatically improved. Use the technology for writing papers or reading school assignments. And if the voice recognition is too disruptive in the classroom, at least allow the student to type directly into a computer or tablet instead of physically writing things out, especially on tests. The autocorrect feature can ease getting the correct information on paper. The calendar feature on the phone is a helpful tool too. Our son was told that technology was not an option. The school policy was no phones or computers in the classroom for anyone. Insist on having technology as an accommodation since it is a vital part of your child's success. Either they change their policy or consider switching schools.

Drill sight words with your early reader. Dyslexic children are usually great at memorizing. If they can quickly identify their sight words, it will give them the self-esteem to figure out some of the other words. Use multi-sensory techniques to assist with the endeavor. Physically have them act out their word. Have them jump, run, or play when you use flashcards for that word. It is much harder for words that don't have a picture associated with it. Where or were, for example, are difficult to differentiate. We would have our child blow on their arm when they said the word. Where has a breath, were does not. A word that confused our son for the longest time was "why." He didn't understand why there were three letters for saying the letter "y." At 28, he still cannot spell the word "queue." Autocorrect is not always a friend.

A small class size of 18 or less is a must-have accommodation. A teacher can observe much more of what is going on in a classroom and assist when necessary. In 4th grade, our youngest son had 14 children in a class with him. His teacher was trained in learning differences, and he had a learning expert who worked with him individually on specific reading techniques for dyslexia. Needless to say, he had a great year.

On the other hand, when our oldest was in 4th grade, he had 30 children in his classroom. He had a teacher with 30 plus years of experience, but none around learning differences. When they had science class, the size doubled to 60 children since they combined two classes. Our son began failing in his favorite subject, science. Class size makes a difference.

A school that uses a variety of instruction methods makes a difference. I already mentioned that multi-sensory learning is helpful, but experimenting with how your child learns best is essential. Writing out words in the sand is a fabulous multi-sensory experience but is not the only accommodation. A teacher needs to be aware of how they explain something to a student, so they understand. I know our youngest son's teacher would always tell us how she would explain something to the class. Everyone would nod that they understood except our son, who would look confused. She would explain it a little differently than our son would understand, but sometimes the other kids would look confused. It could be a word she used he didn't understand, or just conceptually, he was on a different page.

Use the OpenDyslexic font instead of other more difficult-to-read fonts. The OpenDyslexic font is a free typeface/font designed to mitigate some of the expected reading errors caused by dyslexia. Some experts argue it doesn't help. Having two dyslexic children that say it does help would have me question the "experts." My adult children explained how it grounds the letters, so they don't jump around the page. My oldest even installed the font to his browser, so everything he reads is in that font. I am not claiming that your child can instantly read with the font, but I have seen how different fonts caused our boys reading difficulties. For instance, reading a book with all caps was impossible for them. Having the serif fonts is the most difficult for dyslexic children to read. We wrote our book, The

Marshmallow Mystery, in the OpenDyslexic font to encourage early reading and dyslexia awareness.

Knowledge is your superpower. Learn about all the ways to accommodate your dyslexic child. If you would like more resources, go to our website www.cjcorki.com.

FUN THINGS TO DO

Talk:

Chat about their passions and hobbies outside of school. Help them see the connection between their interests and their education. Encourage them to explore how their strengths and passions can be integrated into their academic journey.

Recommend to Read:

- Did You Say Pasghetti? - Tammy Fortune

- What I Need - Tiffany James

- Aaron Slater, Illustrator - Andrea Beaty

Questions to Ask:

What is your favorite part of the school day?

Is there anything that you find challenging at school?

How do you feel when you solve a difficult problem or a task?

CORE VALUE: RESPONSIBILITY

It encompasses a sense of duty, reliability, and the willingness to fulfill commitments as a grandparent.

Stories:

Books:

Questions Asked:

6

Embrace the Struggle: When Learning is Hard

Once freed from archaic schooling practices and preconceptions, my mind opened up. Out in the real world, my dyslexia became my massive advantage.
Richard Branson

Introduction

In addition to the challenges in reading, writing, and spelling, dyslexic children often face various struggles that can significantly impact their educational journey and overall well-being. This invisible disability affects them emotionally for life. Instead of seeing it as a disadvantage, celebrate their gift by considering it a superpower. Their unique way of thinking might cause struggles in school, but they can demonstrate success as they flourish in other areas.

Promote a broader understanding and acceptance of dyslexia within your family, educational system, and society by fostering awareness that embraces all learners' exceptional strengths and abilities. As a grandparent, reassure them that "different" is good. Point out their talents, not their weaknesses. Tell stories about your own struggles and how you overcame them. Create magic in their life. Superior imaginations are part of their superpowers. Be superheroes together.

The Emotional Side of a Learning Difference

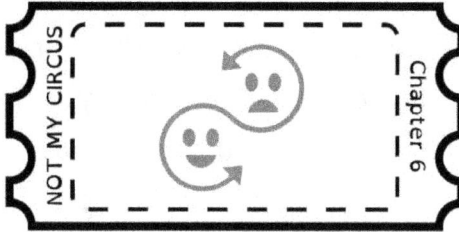

Fact: 35% of dyslexic children don't graduate from high school. Fact: 70% of the people in prison cannot read. It is speculated that the majority of inmates are dyslexic. Learning to read is essential to the well-being of students, not only being successful contributing adults but in their emotional well-being. Not being able to read hurts children's self-esteem leading to depression or worse. These facts alone should have the educational system advocating for the well-being of dyslexic students, but instead, this invisible disability goes undetected. How can parents and teachers support their dyslexic children to avoid a path to failure?

Many teachers and parents believe that their children are just lazy. They may have been advanced in their development since birth but cannot perform in the classroom. They might be able to relay their answer verbally but fail on a test. The conclusion is that they are just lazy. According to the author of The Myth of Laziness, by calling them lazy, you are "condemning them as a human being." "The desire to be productive is universal," says Dr. Levine, "but that drive can often be frustrated by dysfunctions that obstruct output or productivity."

In reality, dyslexic children are working much harder than their peers. They are generally more tired at the end of the day because everything requires more cognitive energy, tasks take longer, and nothing comes easily. More errors are likely to be made, forcing them to go back and correct their mistake, thus taking longer on assignments. One solution is to lighten their academic load. Instead of 20 spelling words, have them learn ten keywords. Let them read a little bit shorter books instead of the longer books their peers are reading. Although this sounds like reasonable accommodations, our youngest son wanted nothing to do with a lighter load. He didn't want to be different from his friends since they would notice.

Dyslexic children feel like they stick out in class. Their reading is labored, so having them read out loud without preparing ahead of time is torture to the student. Our son's 4th-grade class gave peer spelling tests. Each student would ask the other to spell from a list. Not only was it challenging for our son to read the words he wasn't familiar with, but his spelling was also so bad that the other student thought he was dumb. Most people with dyslexia have a higher-than-average IQ. And dyslexia is more common in gifted children. But if you were to ask a dyslexic student that question, they would say they are dumb. They feel that way since they don't excel in school like their peers. It is frustrating to a student who is bright and capable of getting low grades on tests. Our son would hide his grades from his high-achieving friends. They would get A's, and he would be lucky to get a C with a lot of hard work.

To give them hope, we suggest you use examples of highly successful people who struggled in school. Listen to Stephen Spielberg's story about his difficulties with academics and the teasing that accompanied it. Other successful dyslexics are Steve Jobs, Magic Johnson, John Lennon, Albert Einstein, Leonardo da Vinci and more.

Henry Winkler, an actor in Happy Days, started a series of children's books, The World's Greatest Underachiever. He captures his struggles with dyslexia as a fun way for children to understand their struggles. In his newest book, Fake Snakes and Weird Wizards, Winkler uses the dyslexic font, which helps dyslexic and non-dyslexic readers to read more easily.

In CJ Corki's first book in the Can You Find, Did You Know series, we used the dyslexic font to help young readers and to bring dyslexia awareness to parents and teachers. For more book recommendations, go to CJ Corki.com/dyslexia-resources.

If I Only Knew it was a Superpower

When our oldest was born, I quickly started him on a path toward the love of books. Just weeks old, I would prop him up on my lap to recite Dr. Suess's, One Fish, Two Fish, Red Fish, Blue Fish. We progressed to Good Night Moon where I would point out the kittens and the mittens to identify objects in the room. By the age of two, he could "read" the Polar Express word for word. Barney was never part of his repertoire; however, Brontosaurus and Brachiosaurs became part of his vocabulary early on. As a proud parent, I highlighted his precociousness to family and friends. He soared through his preschool absorbing the educational play time like a sponge. When he started kindergarten, he quickly became the teacher's pet. In first grade he was one of two students in his class identified for the gifted program. Dreams of a doctor, lawyer or engineer became part of our expectations for his future. But our hopes vanished as he entered fourth grade, the turning point in his education.

When our son started a new school in the affluent suburb of Chicago, his gifted status was ignored. His teacher with thirty plus years' experience looked at him with distain as he fidgeted in his seat seemingly bored with the curriculum. When he took the achievement test in science, his favorite subject, the results were dismal. He began hiding his assignments and tests from me and the teacher since he no longer had the stars and smiley faces on the paper, but D's and F's. The vibrant, happy child with the passion for learning, disappeared. Meeting after meeting with the teachers and advisors, they concluded he was suffering from depression. I was off to what was the first of many rounds of psychologists and specialists to "fix" the problem.

Take him to a couple of psychological sessions and boom, all is well with the world or so I thought. Yes, it was determined he was depressed. We just moved from a small town in Nebraska to a big metropolis. He left all his friends without the ability to say good-bye. Surely it was the depression that was causing his academic failings. But nothing seemed to work to help his situation. Simultaneously, his little brother was in first grade struggling with reading. His teacher wanted him in "Reading Recovery" which she assured me would be temporary since he was so smart. But to everyone's surprise, he did not improve. So now, there were two of our children struggling at school. My failing as a parent in the eyes of the school was frustrating. I was determined to find an answer to their reading dilemma.

By nature, I am a problem solver. My research gene kicked in to solve the mystery. After hours of internet time learning about parental rights, I went to the school administration armed with a written request to test our oldest son for possible learning disabilities. Although they initially pushed back, they eventually complied.

When reviewing the results, they were shocked to find that his IQ was in the gifted range while his reading level was only at the second-grade level. Although I felt it was low for a gifted fourth grader, they felt it was still in the normal range. Assuring me this could be solved with some specialized assistance from teachers, they sent me on my way. But I was not convinced.

Although I had no background in teaching or learning disabilities, my gut said something is wrong. I found an independent psychologist to re-test our son. When the results came back, we were relieved to find an answer, however, understanding the challenges ahead were foggy to say the least. It was determined he had Dyslexia and Dysgraphia. Not only reading, but writing would be a forever impediment in his educational development, so we were told. But since we now had a diagnosis, the options became clear.

The recommendation was to home school him, but as I mentioned, that ability is not in my repertoire. Sending him away to a school which specialized in dyslexia was cost prohibitive. One thing I did know for sure, he was not staying in the public school system which tried to sweep the issue under the rug. We were on the hunt for other choices. After visiting the gifted schools and private schools, we decided the private route which gave us the ability to put all the boys in the same school. Both boys with reading challenges would get the benefit of the smaller classroom as well as our middle son who was a voracious reader. Problem solved?

Actually, it was not that easy. It was a full-time job to be his advocate for this seemingly invisible disability. His giftedness had him score A's on tests only to fail the next. The rollercoaster ride of getting him to graduate high school was nothing short of exhausting for all of us. But one day, I ran across a book called, The Dyslexic Advantage. It was a paradigm shift in understanding. Dyslexia in the teacher's eyes, as well as mine, was seen as an obstacle. In reality, it was a superpower. Although the struggle is real to learn to read, their ability to compensate developed other abilities. Due to their unique brain structure, and organization, they have the talent to achieve things greater than the non-dyslexics. The science shows that they use more of their brain function than an average person. It is actually a diagnosis you want your child to have.

Going through the challenges of raising two dyslexic children is something I would not wish for any parent, until now. If I only knew in the beginning the creativity that comes through in their development. Instead of trying to "fix" the problem, I should have tried to celebrate their ability and talents. Even though the oldest did not make it through college, he is a successful self-taught computer architect. Our youngest is now finishing his MBA from Case Western. He is maintaining a 4.0 GPA while working fulltime. Do not get me wrong, it will be a struggle to get a dyslexic child through school, but the benefit for their future success is well worth the effort. Remember, it is your child's superpower.

What are your challenges raising a child with learning differences?

Second Language Dilemma:
Do the Benefits Out Way the Damage

No entiendo Española. Je ne comprends pas le français. Nie rozumiem. Non capisco. This is the extent of my rigorous training and immersion into various languages: Spanish, French, Polish, and Italian. I can confidently say I don't understand in all four languages. It isn't as though I didn't try. My schooling started when I attended Head Start at three years old. I came home spouting all sorts of Spanish words from what I was told. But my linguistic talents went downhill after that. While playing a language game with my sister and cousin, I mistranslated a picture of someone pointing to their teeth as "How are your teeth." Yes, an absurd translation that they never let me forget. My forte wasn't languages. I muddled through my language and English classes, but I excelled in math, leading me into engineering. Nobody questioned my language challenges since; overall, I was a good student. But this isn't the case for children with dyslexia. The inability to learn a language besides English should be a red flag for parents.

It is unusual to start learning another language before high school in our public school system. Although many studies show significant benefits to raising a bilingual child, our system isn't set up for the experience. When we pulled our children out of public schools into a private school environment, French was taught as early as 1st grade. It was conversational French which isn't as rigorous as reading and writing in a different language. However, our dyslexic children struggled. They were stressed by learning their primary language, English, so adding another language into the mix was not beneficial. Little did I know that French is a very difficult language to learn, like English. Spanish would have been a better choice since it is a more straightforward and predictive language.

As our boys continued through their school years, they were introduced to Latin. Studying Latin, a highly organized and logical language, much like studying math, sharpens the mind or the school thought. Our son got the idea of adding the various suffixes to words that he knew to understand the language. It wasn't successful. The result was nonsensical language that would not get a passing grade.

Once they entered high school, it was required to take a language to apply to college. After trying French, Spanish, and Latin, we weren't hopeful about the choices. Two years in one language would destroy any decent GPA, most likely prohibiting them from any college anyway. But we took the poor guidance from the counselors and forged ahead. Our oldest tried learning Chinese. This language wasn't a wrong choice since the words were all pictures. He excelled in the printed version; however, conversational Chinese was a disaster. Although he did get an opportunity to visit China with his class, that was the only positive experience from the course.

Another school transfer brought our boys back into the public schools. The language requirement offered sign language. Even though the counselors warned that sign language would not qualify for most college admission requirements, the guidance turned out to be inaccurate. They were able to get a respectable B grade for their two years in the classes. College admissions didn't blink. They did not apply to the Ivy League colleges, but they were accepted nonetheless in good schools.

Unfortunately, the language saga didn't end there. In college, our youngest was required to take a language to graduate. He could opt-out to an even more punitive class for a dyslexic student, so he forged ahead and took Swahili instead. He did contemplate taking Spanish since his girlfriend was fluent in the language and offered to tutor him, but we advised against a potentially high-stress experience.

The academic environment can site studies on how learning a language can benefit a student. However, even though I could be considered a good student, learning a second language was more damaging than productive. Math served me as a second language, and I excelled. I am envious of those who know another language, but I am now comfortable with my limits. This was not the case in high school, where I felt very inept in French. The C grades damaged my grade point average. It only served as a "check the box" for college applications. My experience is only magnified if I was dyslexic.

When we tested our son in fourth grade for learning disabilities, it was noted that he should be exempt from learning another language. This fact was ignored his entire academic career. Teachers and counselors who "knew better" told us to continue with classes that we're destroying our children's self-esteem. The aggravation did not out way the benefits. What is the solution? Awareness! We are promoting dyslexia awareness for parents, teachers, and students. Join the cause.

Teacher's Purpose is to Have Students Succeed, Not Fail

Now that children are returning to school, I think back to the stress of starting the new year for our family. Everyone is excited, but the teachers are not always familiar with their new students. They may have received notes from the prior year's teacher, but not in our case. We moved around the country when the boys were little. Our boys had a different school (and the teacher) almost every year from 3 years old pre-school until sixth grade. These were critical years to learn to read. But teachers want their students to flourish and support those who work hard to achieve success. It wasn't until our oldest son was in fourth grade that he started failing at school. Teachers thought he was lazy, but he was actually dyslexic and gifted too.

The hypocritic oath of "do no harm" should be something that teachers pledge for their students. It is easy for a teacher who teaches to hard-working students whose learning style matches how they teach. But when the student doesn't learn, only the child suffers. A competent veteran teacher of 30 years did not notice the signs of dyslexia. She said our son was lazy or maybe depressed since we just moved to the big city of Chicago from Nebraska. Indeed, they thought, our boys were lagging because of poor teaching back in the small-town USA. Our son may have been a straight-A gifted student back there, but the big city had better teaching methods. Or so they thought.

As a "just fix it" parent, I promptly took him to a psychologist, where they diagnosed him with depression. Looking back, of course, he would be depressed since he was failing at school. In prior years he was the teacher's pet. He was always willing to help, especially if technology was required. He would fix the projector, audio, or any issue a teacher needed assistance doing. He stayed after class to clean the chalkboard or straighten up the classroom. His pleasant smile was now crushed by consistent failure at the school.

At this same time, our youngest son was in first grade. He was having a problem reading. They called me into a teacher's conference recommending he participates in "Reading Recovery." The teacher recognized he was very smart, so she assured me he would be in the program only for a short time. It was most likely because of his "lack of education" in the schools in Nebraska. Or they thought that I was not modeling good reading behavior at home. He just needed a little extra help, they said. But by the end of the year, the program didn't work, and he still couldn't read.

By this time, I was up to my eyeballs in research on the internet. I learned about my rights as a parent to request an evaluation. The school balked about doing this when they were so busy at the end of the year, but I was determined. They complied with the assessment but refused services because he was in the "range" of an average student. Who would have guessed two years behind is "normal" even for a gifted student? It was not over.

We went to an outside psychologist for an unbiased evaluation. The results concluded our oldest son had dyslexia and dysgraphia, problems with reading and writing. Based on these results, our youngest son, we found, had similar symptoms of dyslexia. Their recommended solution...homeschooling. She explained that they would not be successful in the typical public-school forum. Teachers who didn't have a background in learning differences would not know how to teach someone with extreme abilities for both gifted skills and dyslexic challenges.

Homeschooling was not an option, but neither was doing nothing. We searched for another school for all three children. Interviews at gifted schools, dyslexic-specific schools, and private schools came into play. Our goal answered the following question, "are your teachers' dyslexia aware and trained?" Although our middle son does not have these challenges, having a school aware of the array of learning differences would make a difference for all of them.

In 2001, the controversial book came out, Coloring Outside the Lines by Roger Schank. Roger believes that every day of the school year, our children are being failed by an academic system that does nothing to stir a lifelong passion for learning. So, what happened to the teachers' purpose of successful learning? Even worse, the "do no harm" philosophy for our students. Instead of training teachers on Critical Race Theory, how about Dyslexia Awareness? For African American and Latino students, their dyslexia challenges are primarily undiagnosed. If we can teach everyone to read, their likely hood of success will follow. This awareness alone would have a win-win for both teacher and student. It would fulfill the teacher's purpose for students to go to school to succeed, not fail.

My story of our children's struggles will continue for future generations unless we bring awareness to everyone. Teacher's jobs are hard, but the failure of our children shouldn't be an option.

Dyslexia Isn't Something You Outgrow

Teachers often say your child will outgrow some of their issues with reading, writing, or arithmetic. School administrators will require testing every five years to validate the need for accommodations. In reality, students learn to compensate for their dyslexia, but they never outgrow it. I call it the invisible disability. It may seem that your child is performing well in school at the beginning of the year resulting in the "need" for accommodations being overlooked. Maybe extra time on tests is seen as unnecessary or considered an advantage for that student. If your child has issues in first grade, they will continue through college and into adulthood.

As a first grader, a dyslexic student might have the accommodation of not being required to read out loud unless they have a chance to prepare for it. They would need to practice reading the passage to see if there are any unknown words. In college, the same accommodation should be allowed to continue. Our youngest son attended a liberal arts university. His freshman English teacher required each student to read a passage randomly. When she called on him, he said he would pass on reading. After class, the teacher pulled him aside to ask why. He explained he is not comfortable reading random passages since he would be concerned, he would sound like a first-grader. He went on to explain that he has dyslexia. She asked for his accommodations paperwork which he did not have the first week of school. The college required him to get retested since it was more than five years since the last assessment showed the learning difference. Our son had the accommodation not to read aloud since first grade, but the perception was that he should have grown out of it by college. Would you expect a blind person to read from a typical book or someone in a wheelchair to be able to walk? Why is dyslexia not looked at in the same way? Reading aloud is difficult in first grade and continues through college for a person with dyslexia.

Being exempt from learning another language has been our boys' accommodation since they were first assessed with dyslexia in first grade as well. When we switched to a private elementary school, the curriculum included French. Since it was "conversational" at this point, they muddled through it. We moved to a different city in middle school, and the curriculum not only had French but also required Latin. At this point, it was mandatory to read and write in foreign languages. No matter how hard I pressed as a concerned parent, they stood by their language obligations until I pulled them into the public school for high school. At this point, the discussion centered around college preparation. According to the counselors, the boys would need two years of a language to be considered for any college. It was evident that college admissions would not take our paperwork about a known disability. Fortunately, the high school offered sign language as an option. Even though counselors said many colleges would not accept sign language instead of Spanish, French, Latin, or other languages, they did. But once our boys were accepted into college, there still was a language requirement. Again, they did not accept the documented learning disability. Either take a language or a crazy hard alternative meant to "punish" those opting out of a language.

Having extra time is an accommodation necessary for people with dyslexia to do well on tests. It is a proven fact that people without dyslexia do not do any better when given extra time. To a dyslexic student, it evens the playing field. Our son has been offered extra time for exams in first grade through high school. However, when he requested extra time on the ACT, we jumped through hoops to get the accommodation. Even though he met the requirements, he was denied. He muddled through to get a respectable score to qualify him for college and the NCAA constraints for playing soccer. His next barrier was graduate school and taking the GMAT. His preferred college required a minimum test score with no extra time allowed and no waiver for his disability. This time, studying for the test decreased the score instead of increasing it. Admissions saw the GMAT score as an absolute measure for success in getting an MBA. He was denied admissions for the full-time program but accepted into the part-time program. He graduated with a 3.98 GPA, proving that the GMAT should not have been the barrier for entrance, especially when extra time on the test was again denied.

Having a note taker is a needed accommodation for a dyslexic student. Our son required this assistance in grade school and high school, but it didn't stop there. When he went to college, the learning disability department put the burden back on the student for arranging any accommodations. The responsibility entailed talking to the teacher after the first class to ask for a notetaker, extra time on tests, etc. The teacher would then ask my son to find a notetaker to meet that part of the requirements. The process was an embarrassing event since other students were around and they didn't understand dyslexia. He, in turn, didn't ask for the accommodations. It wasn't until his junior year that he finally got things sorted out, which caused his grades to suffer.

As a parent, we are advocates for our children until college. As adults, dyslexic students need to learn self-advocation. But an even better solution is for parents and grandparents to join the information age on dyslexia awareness. From students to adulthood, everyone should be uninhibited in learning to read.

FUN THINGS TO DO

Talk:

Explain that dyslexia often comes with unique strengths and abilities. Many people with dyslexia are creative, have excellent problem-solving skills, think outside the box, and have strong visual and spatial reasoning. Share examples of famous individuals with dyslexia who have achieved great success, such as artists, entrepreneurs, or inventors.

Recommend to Read:

- Magnificent Meg: A Read-Aloud Book to Encourage Children with Dyslexia - Andra Harris

- Finding My Superpower: A book for dyslexic thinkers - Sarah Prestidge

- The Map Challenge: A Book about Dyslexia - Tracy Packiam Alloway

Questions to Ask:

How do you feel when you walk into your classroom every morning?

What is your favorite subject or activity in school?

Is there anything you would like to learn more about?

CORE VALUE: OPTIMISIM

A positive and hopeful outlook on life, situations, and the future of your grandchildren's learning differences as a superpower.

Stories:

Books:

Questions Asked:

7

Adventures in Learning

"An adventure a day keeps the routine away." – Jon Miksis

Introduction

Our grandkids are fearless explorers, open to trying new things, and ready to learn from us as they continue to grow every day. Education goes beyond the boundaries of traditional classrooms, and you are one of its teachers. It's an exciting journey that knows no bounds, and we're here to help you make that journey thrilling for everyone.

In this chapter we will help you tap into experiences outside their normal day to day activities as you take them into uncharted territories, help them uncover hidden treasures of knowledge, and watch as their young minds flourish.

So, fasten your seatbelts, get ready to open their minds for a thrilling expedition into the realm of knowledge that only you can provide. Welcome to a world where learning is an adventure like no other!

Playtime is Serious Business

"Play is often **talked about as if it were a relief from serious learning.** But for children, play is serious learning. Play is really the work of childhood," Fred Rogers, aka Mr. Rogers. Children need various types of daily play to support meaningful learning opportunities as they develop language, social, emotional, and cognitive abilities. The types of play include physical, dramatic, sensory, music and art, nature, and age-appropriate play.

Everyday household objects are some of the best toys for babies, toddlers, and preschoolers. These items allow them to explore and encourage their imaginations. Babies are fascinated by their surroundings, especially faces and bright colors, and it's as simple as them grasping an object and holding on to it. Parents and Grandparents can focus on introducing things that stimulate curiosity, like a game of peek-a-boo. For toddlers, look for objects that encourage problem-solving and imagination as they may begin to arrange objects, which eventually turns into sorting and classifying them. For preschoolers, look to use objects to help them relate to each other and the world around them. Encourage their imagination by creating tents made from blankets draped over couches and chairs.

Grandparents are some of the luckiest people I know. My question is, how can you and your grandchild reap all the incredible benefits of your unique relationship in the playtime department? Grandparents can be a friend and fun-loving playmates in the lives of their grandchildren, and their grandchildren will love and remember them for it! Here are some ideas to connect with grandkids at any age; go to the park or movies, take the time to engage in imaginative play, and enjoy the energy of your grandchildren, no matter what they may be up to.

Share what you played as a child. Did you play hopscotch? Was the hula-hoop a thing in your past? Games like Scrabble, hide-and-seek, and Play-Doh are games that your grandchildren would enjoy. Purchase a hula-hoop or two, a couple of board games, and any supplies like chalk needed to introduce the grandkids to the games you played years ago.

Most importantly, have fun with your grandkids! They grow up fast and will remember the times you played unique games with them. When your grandchildren become grandparents, they will pass it on.

Do you want the grandkids to play with you at every age and stage of their life? Let them choose what you play. Most kids are exposed to technology at a young age in our tech-savvy world, and screen time is ok in moderation. In addition, while playing games, let your grandkids win every once in a while. Of course, it is nice to let them win, but I recommend not making it obvious when you lose on purpose.

The role of grandparents in family life is ever-changing. Grandparents can play many roles, from historian to mentor to child-care provider. Strong intergenerational connections can give grandchildren a sense of security of belonging to the extended family. The degree of grandparents' involvement varies from one household to the next, depending on a variety of circumstances such as proximity to grandchildren, relationship to parents, type of family structure, and health of grandparents.

Get inspired to start some new family traditions with your grandkids. Whether you want to go all out or want some easy things to do together, consider some of these ideas to get a tradition going. Camp out in the backyard for some evening star gazing, create a marshmallow bush for some magical morning fun. Family game night can tie this playtime theme together. What are your playtime options?

Science of Secrets

What secret agent did you want to be like when you were growing up?

James Bond, 007
Secret Agent
Man from Uncle
I Spy
Get Smart
Mission Impossible

I loved the cone-of-silence (Get Smart); as children, we would put a blanket over our heads to mimic it. Under the blanket of silence, we could whisper secrets to each other. Fun memories.

All children love secrets. They always have. We certainly did. As grandparents, many of us remember the decoder ring that we could order from the back of a comic book so we could share secrets with our special friends. What fun! Today's children live online. How can a grandparent connect with them without being part of the online noise, keep their interest, and stimulate learning?

Challenge your grandchildren to communicate with you in code. For example, Morse Code. It encourages them to explore a new alphabet outside their comfort zone. This learning moment has the momentum to allow your grandbabies to communicate with you 'in secret'. Kids will be thrilled. Why code? You and your grandkids can discuss Christmas or birthday presents for their parents without their parents 'listening in' to the conversation.

You don't know Morse Code? Easy. You can use a crib sheet, and your grandchild can use the same. Then you are off to the races with your grandkids sharing secrets. Over time, both of you will become proficient and won't need the crib sheet.

If Morse Code is too intimidating, consider the Caesar Cipher. Children 7 and up find this fun, but even younger children who know the alphabet can enthusiastically embrace it. The Caesar Cipher is a simple substitution cipher where you replace one letter with another, in order. A shift of one letter turns A into B, B into C, C into D, etc.

For example:

Shift: 1
Standard Alphabet:
ABCDEFGHIJKLMNOPQRSTUVWXYZ
Cipher Alphabet:
BCDEFGHIJKLMNOPQRSTUVWXYZA

Original Text: I love you
Secret Code: JMPWFZPV

Fun Fact- Caesar preferred the 3 shift, so A became D, B became E, etc.

You and your grandchild can make a cipher wheel and practice using it together to write secret messages to each other.

Granted, today anyone can find a program online that will translate and decode words to Morse Code and Caesar Ciphers. But spending one-on-one time with your grandchildren teaching them to write in code and conveying the history of Morse Code and ciphers can spark their imagination for covert communication while learning new skills. What kid doesn't aspire to be a secret agent?

Why is this important today?

Cybersecurity and encryption are important parts of our information-dominated world. Through these simple beginner steps of Morse Code and Caesar Ciphers, you are introducing your grandchildren to a critical element of our world and sparking interest in math and computer science.

How are you sparking your grandkids' imaginations to expand their knowledge base into new areas? Cone-of-silence (aka blanket-of-silence)? Secret messages? Writing in code?

Farm to Fork: Unleashing Adventure One Husk at a Time

For years, when we were young, my sisters, I, and a bunch of cousins would go on the greatest of adventures.

Where to? A family farm.

When? Harvest time.

Join me as we embark on an exciting foodie adventure.

As subsistence farmers, our aunt and uncle needed us to help hand-pick the animal corn.

Acres and acres of animal corn. Did I mention many acres of animal corn? Sisters and cousins were quickly taught how to pick the corn, shuck it, and toss it into a pile. We worked row-by-row, picking and shucking. None of us were from farm backgrounds. We lived in town so as children, this was a fun and new adventure. We worked hard most of the morning and happily broke for lunch, a simple fare, sandwiches, pickles, tomato slices and a watermelon for dessert. Packets of chips didn't exist. Bottled water didn't exist. If we were thirsty, we would drink water from the well. Unfortunately, this area of Illinois had well water that contained a lot of sulfur, so it smelled— really smelled! We wrinkled our noses but still drank it, even covered over by a Kool-Aid packet and sugar.

When we finally finished our morning's work, we would ride on the tractor-driven cart to pick up the shucked corn. Our next job was to throw the corn from the ground into the cart's bed. When we finished, we had free time before supper. We happily explored the farm. The pig pen was particularly fun because the mud-drenched pigs oinked and squealed as we climbed the fence to get a closer look. We would grab their tails to see how long we could hang on before we had to let it go. The pigs appeared to expect our behavior and were good with this "city folk" entertainment. We were cautioned not to jump into the pig pen directly because the animals did bite and could be dangerous. Our uncle asked if we wanted to learn how to drive the tractor. Wide-eyed, we all said yes. Luckily or not for me, I was chosen to be the first one. Sigh. My first experience with manual transmission was at the ripe age of 12. I didn't do as well as I thought and almost ran into a post with the tractor. After this experience, driving a manual transmission car was a piece of cake.

I share this because these are valuable childhood memories. Children fondly remember these unique adventures. Years from now, they will not remember playing computer games on their cell phones or watching TikTok videos, but they will remember the unique experience of harvesting food, large quantities of food. More than just picking enough for mom to cook it for dinner but to have enough to last until next year's harvest.

How can we make a memory for our grandchildren? Since most grandparents don't live on family farms, an alternative solution exists. There are many 'pick-your-own' places to take your grandchildren. Participating in this experience can teach the little ones the value of physical labor and, more importantly, persistence. This latter is missing in today's generation. Prior generations of children learned to pick vegetables, pull weeds, and pick cotton for many hours and pretty much mostly for weeks or months. It was an expectation as part of a family. If you have had such experiences, it is time to share them with your grandchildren. How did you feel as a child spending the days in hot sun picking fruit or vegetables? What did that teach you? Transmit these life experiences to your grandchildren. Trust me they will remember your words.

You don't have to make a day of this outdoor experience. If you go to a pick-your-own farm, set a time limit, say 30 minutes, and tell your grandchild/children to pick what they can. No cell phone, no earbud music. Be persistent. Make sure they work for the entire time. It will be a learning moment for both of you. You now have a gauge of your grandchild's attention span. The key is to teach them to extend the span of their concentration on an activity to 30 minutes, not the standard TikTok video of 3 minutes. Once they have worked for 30 minutes, they will be surprised by how many vegetables or fruit they picked. You have now expanded their focused concentration from 3 minutes to 30 minutes. A victory.

So, let's take this to the next level. Once you have the fruit or vegetables that your grandkid(s) have collected and brought back to your kitchen, you can teach them more patience in shucking corn, shelling peas, and cutting off the tops of strawberries. This next step demonstrates the natural process of how food is made. They will experience farm-to-fork. Making the food they like to eat might help them look at the food they typically eat differently. If you have your grandchild(s) sitting on the porch with a bucket of veggies or fruit to prepare them for preserving or canning or freezing, you can use that time as story time. Their hands are busy, so they are not on their cell phones. They have your undivided attention. Tell them stories. Engage them with fairy tales or stories of your youth. Or you can put down your bucket and pick up a storybook and read them a story about children helping parents on a farm or a bible story—your choice.

If canning or freezing or otherwise preserving what your grandchildren have prepared is not your thing, contact your friends. Many may appreciate being provided with an abundance of shucked or pealed food that they can preserve helping their budget moving forward. And maybe, invite them to the shucking party to provide their stories of their past in doing these activities while your grandkids work. Win-win-win.

Teaching the value of hard work is vital for children. This is a life lesson and NOT child labor; it teaches our children to use their hands to accomplish much in their life, see the value of their work, and feel self-satisfied and that there is personal accomplishment woven into work done well.

Let's help them savor the taste of hard work in every bite! Adventure awaits, take the grandkids along for the ride!

Let's Have a Ball

Unplug their thumbs, train their mind, and body and unleash their full potential...

It's no secret that kids today are growing up spending more time than ever before indoors, glued to screens and finger-driven devices. Their finger/eye coordination abilities are off the chart, but what about old-fashioned hand-eye coordination that requires more than a finger and gives them a pause from their fingers?

Here is an activity we can do with our grandchildren that doesn't require a computer-driven device:

Paddleboard

Remember these? A flat panel with a stapled elastic band to its center connected to a quarter-size red ball. The objective is to hit the ball on the paddle and then hit it again when it comes back. Sounds easy-peasy, doesn't it? But do you remember taking this to the next level?

1. Instead of hitting the ball horizontally, can you do it fast vertically, either up in the air or down to the ground?

2. Fast competitions with your friends. How fast can you hit the ball when it returns within 1 minute?

3. Acrobatic competition. Can you hit the ball with the paddle while hitting the ball under your arm or leg? This level allows the child to use their brain to figure out more challenging activities for mastering the paddle board. This is where you ultimately want to be. Your grandchildren have engaged their brains to coordinate hand/eye and learn to develop strategies to do physical activity.

Get these for your grandkids and one for yourself and show them how to use it. Once they have eye/hand coordination and the suggestions of competition, you can leave them with their paddle board in the backyard and let them figure out other ways to use this toy. After they have had time to play with this challenging toy, let them challenge you to a competition of their choice. A win-win. They have developed a hand-eye coordination skill, honed it, and you have challenged their mind to create more difficult paddling exercises to challenge you, their grandparent.

Oh, and guess what, they have forgotten about their cell phone or another computer-based device as they work to master a physical activity with a challenge to 'an old person' to something that the 'old person' grew up doing.

Note to self: Practice before introducing the paddleboard to my grandchildren. YES, this IS a competition. Be prepared to take your grandchildren on. It is not for you to win but to motivate them to get off their devices and use their brains to take up a challenge with their physical activity.

Just remember, if you win, you win. Your grandchild doesn't need a participation trophy. They will respect you more, knowing you can beat them and maybe spur them to hone their skills for a rematch. Total win-win. You accomplished your goal: Get them to do something other than a computer device and encourage their competitive nature to improve their performance in the real world, not the digital one.

Winning is good, but losing teaches. Hand-eye coordination for the win!

Comfort Food of the Past: Grandparent's Role in Expanding Kids' Horizon

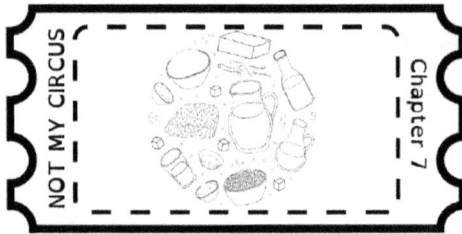

NOT MY CIRCUS | Chapter 7

There was nothing better than a plate of warm, juicy sausage smothered in tangy sauerkraut. It always made me feel at home and brought back memories of cozy family dinners. What about you? What was your favorite comfort food when you were a child? Mac and Cheese? Sloppy Joe's? Meatloaf? French Fries? Something else?

For me, it was Polish sausage and sauerkraut. My Busha (a diminutive form of Polish grandmother, but we called her Bushi) was the best cook in the universe. Walking into her house was like walking into heaven. The smell of sauerkraut simmering on the stove permeated the house all the time. Bushi made a full range of Polish food, from pierogi to potica (translation here—pierogi is like Polish ravioli, and potica is a nut roll pastry, which is to die for.)

Another food that I enjoy is called czernina (pronounced: CHAR-nina), one of the oldest Polish soups. My Busha would make this when the butcher got in a load of ducks. The key ingredient of this soup is duck blood.

Yes. Seriously. Ducks. Blood.

It is honestly delicious. I've talked with friends whose grandmothers made czernina, and they remember their Bushi telling them it was 'chocolate soup,' and they believed it pretty much like believing in the Easter Bunny. They liked it until they learned the ingredients. Oh well.

Fast forward to today. What do your grandchildren like to eat? My guess is chicken nuggets. That is today's comfort food for our grandkids. It is understandable as it can be eaten with their fingers and easily ordered at any restaurant on this planet.

How do you introduce new food to your grandchildren? Or do you?

It is so hard when we have our grandkids for a weekend (or week). We want them to have a good and memorable time. As grandparents, we want to pamper them, but we realize this is also an opportunity to expose them to new gastronomical experiences.

Now, I am not necessarily recommending this but...my Busha never asked us what we wanted to eat for breakfast/lunch/dinner. She put a plate in front of us and expected us to eat what she had made. If we didn't eat it, we went hungry.

Did you ever hear the comment, "Remember the "starving children in Poland/Africa/everywhere else in the world?" That was thrown at me and my sisters who refused to try something new or not eat what was given to us.

So, should we return to expecting children to eat what we put in front of them or let them control the narrative?

This is a tricky question for grandparents who want their grandkids' experiences to be positive when they are visiting.

How do you handle fussy eaters in your house? How would you entice a child to try czernina? (seriously, this is a delicious soup!).

I must ask: "Are we limiting our grandkids' food horizon?" Are we limiting our grandkids' innate curiosity about the world around us, including food?

Shouldn't we strive to give our kids the same opportunity to explore other cuisines and flavors as we did growing up? We should strive to introduce our grandkids to more diverse food choices by exposing them to different cultures and cuisines.

I believe that it's up to us as grandparents to encourage kids to explore new flavors and ingredients and give them a chance to sample dishes that may have been part of our past.

The key here is to get creative!

Start by introducing one new food at a time, and make sure to describe the food's taste, smell, and texture beforehand.

I suggest dessert since most children are drawn to sweets. Candied pecans maybe, a Southern favorite. Or be a little more adventurous with candied hibiscus flowers (an Arabic favorite). Even just candied dates. Or how about a chocolate croissant (French favorite). Each has a distinct texture and flavor. The pecan may not be far from their experience with pecan pie. Chocolate croissant would be like a chocolate donut. The other two are simply sweet. Get them to trust that trying new things can be tasty.

Letting kids explore different ingredients and tastes on their own terms will help them develop healthy eating habits and prevent fussy eating habits from forming early on. Don't forget that including family favorites can also help bridge any gaps between food choices from different generations; it's also a great way to teach kids about cultural traditions and the importance of sharing meals with family.

Ask questions throughout the meal, like "Do you like it?" or "How would you rate it?" Allow your grandchild enough time to try the new food without pressure—you may even lead by example by eating some yourself! You could also turn mealtimes into educational opportunities by discussing where certain foods come from, their nutritional benefits, and even some fun facts about them. By doing this, you can make mealtime an enjoyable experience for everyone involved!

We should also take advantage of opportunities, such as international events or multicultural festivals where kids can explore flavors from different countries without having to leave home. We should also look for ways to involve kids in meal preparation, so they get excited about the process, even if the final product isn't something they usually enjoy. It's about giving access to different types of cuisine and fostering an attitude of exploration, so they are always open to trying something new.

Maybe Polish 'chocolate soup,' (czernina) will be the next comfort food. Quack.

No Boredom for Kiddos at Grandma's Camp

Choosing a name for your camp is a personal decision, but many grandparents opt for a generic name like "Grandma's Camp" or "Grandpa's Camp," or they may personalize it by using their name. My parents called theirs Camp Cadillac for their grandkids at their lake house in Illinois. Before retirement, my parents dreamed of owning a Cadillac and afterward, they were happy to own several. "Camp Cadillac" is a nod to their post-retirement ownership of several Cadillac cars.

There are many boredom busters that you can have ready for your grandchildren, such as craft supplies, board games, outdoor activities, books, and puzzles. You can also consider planning a special outing or activity, like a trip to the park or museum or a movie day. It's important to have a variety of options to keep them engaged and entertained. Spending quality time with grandparents can create lasting memories for children.

Grandma's Camp is usually held during the summer, but some grandparents also choose to hold it during spring break or Christmas break. The duration of Grandma's Camp should be carefully considered, especially if it's your first time organizing it. It's recommended to start with a short and manageable duration before gradually increasing it.

Grandma Camps are usually 2-3 days long, but they can last up to a week. It's best to choose a shorter duration unless the grandchildren are older and self-sufficient. Make sure to announce the date early so family members can plan accordingly. If you don't have enough beds for your grandchildren, air mattresses or foam pieces that can be rolled up and stored are good solutions. Using sleeping bags can also reduce the amount of bedding you need to supply and launder. For very young campers, a portable crib and appropriate bedding that excludes pillows, comforters, or blankets are necessary for a safe sleep environment. Setting up a tent in the yard can be a fun option if the weather permits, but always make sure at least one adult stays with the children.

When planning meals for your campers, it's helpful to get a list of foods they will eat ahead of time. Try to come up with menus that will appeal to most of your guests, while upholding nutritional standards. Planning and doing food prep can make meals easier, and ordering pizza or using paper plates with names can reduce clean-up time. Eating outdoors can also add a festive touch. Having a theme for a camp can make it more enjoyable and ideas tend to flow easily once you settle on one. However, it's important not to overdo it with decorations and focus more on using the theme to organize activities.

Here are some theme ideas for your camp. Travel: Explore different countries and cultures. Fantasy: Create your magical world inspired by books or movies like Harry Potter or Lord of the Rings. Nature: Animals, plants, and geology.

Fatigue can be a challenge for grandparents spending time with their grandchildren. To avoid exhaustion, it's recommended to start well-rested, take breaks throughout the day, and even require rest periods for the children. With older children, you can explain the need to rest and have them wait on you. Remember to take care of yourself so you can fully enjoy the time with your grandkids.

The Elevator to Success is Out of Order, So What Happens Next?

You have to use the stairs!

No, this blog isn't about taking the stairs to avoid the elevator Muzak, now called Mood Media, commonly found in elevators. So why am I writing about elevators? Because we are a society that revels in instant gratification. Humor me as I talk about the early days when the hottest technology was using a fax machine that was used to send documents electronically over a telephone network. After waiting 30 minutes you would call the recipient to confirm that they received the document. Fax machines have gone the way of the dinosaur.

Today if asked, are you hungry? Call Uber Eats. Want something tomorrow? You don't even have to leave your house Amazon will have it there! Sometimes we want something instantly when it would be better for it to have happened more slowly.

Because our grandkids are a source of joy, pride and love I am sharing the idea that maybe we help them feel that tingle of excitement about what they do, sticking with important things through hard times, and living a life they can be proud. Every generation comes in under the influences of the generations before it. The influences of prior generations, us, can teach them that achievement takes a plan, that patience is worth the wait, and maybe that taking the long way, or the right stairs, will earn their success.

So, let's rally to help motivate our grandkids. We know what it was like, early in their childhood; trying something new was easy. Since we live in a "need it now" society, it can be challenging for us to know how to help them stay motivated and engaged for the long ride.

The first step in my unofficial playbook is to help them to try new things and get them out of their comfort zone. Our goal should be to enable them to accept "leaning into discomfort" and develop skills that will help them in the future. Here are a few tips to help our grandkids find motivation and enjoy life.

Encourage Them to Find a Job

Jobs are a good thing. We all have had one or two in our lifetime, and we know what freedom, responsibility, and having our own money feel like. Don't let them pass up this great life lesson. If your grandkid is interested in specific fields, encourage them to explore them. They get real-world experience while taking on more responsibility - which looks great on resumes. These experiences also help kids learn valuable skills such as problem-solving and communication that will help them later.

Set Realistic Goals

We all need goals if we want our lives to have meaning; however, setting too many lofty goals can overwhelm anyone. It is better for you to sit down with your grandchild and come up with realistic goals they can work towards over time instead of trying to accomplish everything immediately. These goals should be tailored around what they want to do in the long term - whether it's what they want to be doing in 10 years or learning a new skill. This will give them something positive and tangible they can work towards while still having fun!

Remember, we are in this for the long haul. Following up with them while they are learning the skill of holding themselves accountable to attaining those goals. A weekly follow up asking for an update might be just what they need to keep moving forward.

Try New Things Together

Try different activities together – take a cooking class or see an art exhibit at a local museum. Doing these types of activities will challenge you and your grandkids out of their comfort zones together but create unforgettable memories at the same time! It also teaches them the importance of trying new things even if it may feel uncomfortable at first - something that could benefit them later in life if they ever find themselves stuck in a rut.

While this may seem daunting at first glance, it's ultimately rewarding to see how much these steps positively impact their growth and development.

So, take some time today and start helping them using the stairs, one step at a time.

FUN THINGS TO DO

Talk:

Discuss how each new experience teaches us something valuable. Trying new things helps us understand ourselves better and makes us stronger, smarter, and more confident.

Share that life is full of wonders waiting to be discovered and will expand their world and helps them find what makes them happy.

Recommend to Read:

- Curious George Adventures in Learning by The Learning Company

- A Unicorn, a Dinosaur, and a Shark Walk into a Book by Jonathan Fenske

- The Big Book by Emily Ford

Questions to Ask:

What is something new you would like to try? Why does it interest you?

How can you overcome any fear or nervousness when trying something new?

What do you think you can learn or discover by trying new things?

CORE VALUE: ADVENTURE

To learn something new, you need to try new things and not be afraid to be wrong.

Stories:

Books:

Questions Asked:

CJ Corki, spirited and imaginative writers, draws inspiration from a childhood steeped in captivating storytelling. Drawing from their own experiences as ringmasters of life's unpredictable circus, CJ Corki shares stories, trials, and obstacles through a lens of humor and profound insights into the captivating world of a grandparent's mind.

Through their vivid and relatable storytelling, they invite readers to join in the magic of grandparenting, where love, wisdom, and laughter intertwine. As an author, they cherish the opportunity to touch lives and ignite imaginations, just as their father once did. With the baton of storytelling firmly in hand, they continue the family tradition of transporting readers to extraordinary worlds, bridging generations, and embracing the timeless power of the written word.

So, grab a cozy seat, and immerse yourself in the stories - the circus of joy awaits.

CJ CORKI

Visit us at
cjcorki.com
or
Contact us at
author@cjcorki.com

www.ingramcontent.com/pod-product-compliance
Lightning Source LLC
Chambersburg PA
CBHW070102030426
42335CB00016B/1982